D1437078

BIG RIGS
IN FOR THE LONG HAUL

BIG RIGS
IN FOR THE LONG HAUL

JOHN G. SMITH

Eagle
Editions

A QUANTUM BOOK

Published by Eagle Editions Ltd.
11 Heathfield
Royston
Hertfordshire SG8 5BW

Copyright ©MCMXCIX
Quintet Publishing Ltd.

This edition printed 2002

ISBN 1-86160-520-X

QUMRRT

This book is produced by
Quantum Publishing Ltd
6 Blundell Street
London N7 9BH

Printed in Singapore by
Star Standard Industries (Pte) Ltd.

Picture Credits
p10, *top and middle*, Mercedes-Benz
Classic Archives; p11, 12, 13, 14, 15, 185,
187, Fondation de l'Automobile Marius
Berliet, Lyon, France; p176, Patrick Cotter;
p183, *top*, Ford Motor Co Ltd.

CONTENTS

FOREWORD
TRUCKS FOR DIFFERENT HORIZONS

I once asked Canadian trucker Dale Holman what kept long-haul drivers behind the wheel. The hours are brutal, the pay can be low, and they live in confines that— even with all the comforts on offer—still aren't home. "It's the sunsets," he said. "I've seen sunsets and sunrises on every horizon in North America. It's that stuff, the moments that the tourists never get to see."

It does actually come down to that. Despite the hassles of the job and the inevitable complaints about their treatment by dispatchers and shippers, some truckers wouldn't trade in their keys for the world. To them, it is more than a job. It's a lifestyle. It's a sense of independence that can only be found on the open road. Trucks may be first and foremost tools for a task, but they're also extensions of their owners' personalities.

This book focuses specifically on the trucks: their past, present, and future. It looks at a few examples of equipment that has been stretched to new limits, and offers a glimpse at the possibilities offered by modern engineering.

I have little doubt that most of those people who crack the binding of this book work their days turning the wheels, or simply dream of the possibility. Imagine if you will the draw to the wheel that's shared by those who drive long-haul trucks in other parts of the world.

This book is dedicated to those who turn the wheels, to those who seek those different horizons.

ABOVE Scania began by making bicycles, and now produces top-of-the-range trucks on sale worldwide.

RIGHT A Foden Alpha Range powers across a rain-soaked bridge.

INTRODUCTION
BEASTS OF BURDEN

For Robert Simpson, the idea of owning a truck would have been little more than a publicity stunt. The cart paths that passed for roads in Toronto, Canada, were still dominated by horse-drawn carriages in 1898, and any horseless carriages were still a novelty. But Simpson could boast that he owned his nation's first delivery truck: an electric Number 2 Coach Delivery Wagon built by the U.S.-based Fischer Equipment Company of Chicago, Illinois.

Still, the Fischer was hardly a model of efficiency. Its maximum payload of about 200 pounds was steered by a driver left exposed to the elements on a perch at the front of the truck. The idea of driving in bad weather would have been absurd, even if the narrow wheels could have pulled their way through the mud. And long-distance runs were those that required a trip across the city. The truck's fully charged batteries may have offered enough energy to travel 35 miles over smoothly paved roads, but few such roads were to be found in the Toronto of that era. The truck had to return every noon hour to have its batteries recharged.

Nevertheless Simpson, and entrepreneurs like him showed promise in the idea of using horseless carriages to carry freight. At the dawn of the world's automotive industry, trucks were quick to emerge as the beasts of burden for a modern age.

The work of these pioneers offered just a glimpse of what was to come. Today, road trains crossing the Australian Outback carry gross combination weights approaching 200 tons. Diesel engines, churning out as much as 600 hp and 2,050 lb-ft of torque, are turning the wheels of rigs climbing through the Rocky Mountains. Trucks built with technology from developed nations are powering the emerging economies of the Third World. And the railroads that once dominated the hauling of freight over land have, in many cases, been relegated to second place behind the more flexible abilities of trucks. With Just-In-Time delivery schedules and satellite tracking, trucks are no longer considered a mere means of carrying freight; they're the rolling warehouses that make factory production possible.

In many ways, modern over-the-road tractors have more in common with the cockpits of Boeing jets than their road-based ancestors of only a few decades ago. In-cab computer displays can help monitor engine operating conditions every second; aerodynamic stylings help rigs slice through the wind and cut precious fuel costs; and even the long-haul trucker's sense of isolation is being challenged with the advent of everything from cellular phones to satellite tracking.

But those who love trucks look at them as more than equipment to do a job. There's the vision of romance associated with traveling the open road. There's the sheer power conveyed by the behemoths of the world's highways. There's the look of polished chrome, the smell of diesel exhaust, the deep sound of rumbling engines, and the barking of engine brakes. There is simply the sheer the rush of commanding the power of hundreds of horses.

Despite the attractions, however, the modern trucking industry faces more than its share of challenges. Long-haul runs can force truckers to leave their families thousands of miles behind them. (Runs from Europe through the former Soviet Union can take truckers away from their families for months on end.) And while there may not be a boss telling truckers what to do at a specific moment in time—in the rare moments when communications equipment doesn't squawk—governments around the world are shouting with voices of their own. Much like doting mothers, transportation departments even decide when it's time for a driver to sleep and when it's appropriate to wake up. Then there's the fight to keep equipment up to safety standards and rolling down the highway, the need to monitor axle weights, the taxing requirements of permits, licenses, tickets, and tolls.

A career in trucking is also a battle against the elements. Those pulling through the Australian Outback know about the kicked-up bull dust that envelops their rigs in a moving cloud. In black soil country, the temperature of the sand can reach a scorching 130° Fahrenheit. And a world away, those traveling the ice roads of northern Canada in the dead of winter are often protected by little more than a small heater, sleeping bags, and duct tape strapped over gaps in the cab. Then there is the havoc wreaked on components by blowing sand in the world's deserts, or the sub-zero temperatures of Siberia that give lubricants the consistency of molasses.

Despite all the challenges, however, there are still the moments that pull truckers back to the road. You can find them beyond the scream of shippers and their Just-In-Time delivery deadlines, on the quiet stretches of open highway that are far from the stress of congested traffic. At the wheel, today's truckers can still feel like masters of their domain; like knights of the road. They know how the low rumble of idling diesels takes on a serene quality in the predawn hours of a truck stop. They know what it's like to see the sun set on different horizons. These are the moments that help the road continue its call.

ABOVE Two Peterbilt 330 models on display. Peterbilt continues to make trucks of classic distinction.

A HISTORY OF THE TRUCK

ABOVE   Gottlieb Daimler, b.1834, the father of the modern truck.

ABOVE   Wilhelm Maybach, b.1846, chief designer at Deutz.

ABOVE   Rudolf Diesel, b.1858, inventor of the combustion principle that bears his name.

If the modern truck has a father, it's Gottlieb Daimler. Most of the world had yet to dream about horseless carriages when Daimler joined Nikolaus August Otto in 1872 to build gasoline engines. But Otto's Deutz gas engine factory was a leader in the emerging technology. It was producing a relatively affordable four-stroke gasoline engine as early as 1876, building on the ideas that surrounded the first internal combustion engine built by Jean Joseph Etienne Lenoir in 1860 and the four-cycle engine developed in 1862 by Alphonse Beau du Rochas.

However Daimler had an idea of his own too. He knew that if he could find a way to increase an engine's speed, he could develop an overall package that would be smaller and lighter than stationary models that depended on gas plants for the necessary fuel. Such a design would be more appropriate for powering vehicles. He knew Wilhelm Maybach, the chief designer at Deutz, could make his ideas a reality, and in 1883 the pair built such an engine with a tube ignition system and a method to control the power.

Forever the entrepreneur, Daimler wanted to power anything that moved. First there was a car and a motorboat in 1886. In 1887, there was the trolley car. In 1892, he even offered to develop a "transporter with engine drive" for the Prussian Army Administration. Although the idea was rejected then, its time would come.

Of course, Daimler and Maybach weren't the only engineering minds working with the rapidly developing internal combustion engine. Rudolf Diesel developed the engine to bear his name in 1892, barely outshining a similar engine that was being developed

in England by Herbert Ackroyd-Stuart. At the dawn of the automobile, the first gasoline-powered truck was a chain-driven Panhard et Levassor Chariot à Plateforme that was built at the Panhard Works in Paris, France. (Designed on October 13, 1894, the vehicle, which was 117 inches long with a platform measuring 59 inches, was first driven by chief engineer Monsieur Mayade on February 10, 1895.) In December 1895, a gasoline-driven Peugeot Frères was powered with a Daimler motor capable of carrying 1,000 pounds at 9 1/2 miles per hour, or 650 pounds at 12 miles per hour. And by then the idea of self-propelled vehicles was spreading to North America. Charles E. and J. Frank Duryea established the first U.S. automobile manufacturing company that same year, 1895.

However, until 1895 efforts to build load-carrying vehicles were simply isolated experiments. It was then that Daimler-Motoren-Gesellschaft became the first commercial producers of a truck line with the Daimler-Motor-Lastwagen. The trucks boasted two forward speeds and one reverse, with a twin-cylinder Phoenix engine mounted on the back. A 4-hp model could be used to carry 3,300-pound loads, a 6-hp engine was needed for 5,500-pound weights, there was an 8-hp model for 8,250-pound loads, and a 10-hp one for weights of 11,000 pounds. The 4-hp model could travel 7 1/2 miles per hour, and drivers who were otherwise exposed to the elements

ABOVE The first gasoline-powered truck was a chain-driven Panhard et Lavassor Chariot à Plateforme, built at the Panhard Works in Paris, France. It was first driven in 1895 by Monsieur Mayade, the chief engineer.

LEFT The world's first fully-operational diesel engine, built in 1897.

could even take advantage of an optional heater that drew on cooling water that was heated by the engine and fed through tubes mounted on the driver's box.

Speditions-firm Paul von Maur of Stuttgart, Germany bought the first model in the spring of 1897 and the era of the modern truck was born. A year later, the Winton Company built North America's first gasoline-powered delivery wagon with a design based on a two-cylinder passenger car chassis and incorporating both wire spoke wheels and tiller steering.

If Daimler is to be considered the father of the modern truck, however, Nicolas Joseph Cugnot should be considered its grandfather. Even the French army officer would have had to admit that the cannon mover he built in 1770 looked a little odd. It comprised a pear-shaped copper cauldron mounted in front of a single wheel, with two other wheels trailing to the rear. Without a doubt there was nothing else like it on the road, but it moved without the strength of any animal.

Steam building up in the vehicle's boiler pushed at the piston in one of the two cylinders straddling the front wheel. A rocking beam that was attached to the piston shifted under the force. The piston at the other end of the rocking beam repositioned within its cylinder. And through it all, there was motion through a ratchet. The front wheel rolled forward ... a little too far forward.

Even though the cannon mover couldn't exceed a top speed of about 2½ miles per hour when enough steam built up, there was a distinct control problem. The world's first truck met with the world's first truck accident when it pushed down a section of wall before coming to a halt on its maiden run. Nevertheless steam power wasn't completely discounted in Europe until as late as the 1930s. There were the inherent power-to-weight problems, the agonizing waits for boilers to build up the steam needed to turn a wheel, and the pesky leaks. But for all its faults, steam power still worked.

John Yule relied on steam power in 1870 when he built one of the world's first successfully self-propelled wagons to travel the two-mile trip down the narrow lanes of Rutherglen Loan to the docks in Glasgow, Scotland. It normally took the strength of 400 men to drag his 40-ton marine boilers to their destination. But the truck with a 250-rpm twin-cylinder steam engine mounted on a 26-foot red pine chassis turned its six wheels at three quarters of a mile per hour. And where it would have cost him £60 to hire the men to drag his products down to the dock, his wagon simply burnt fuel valued at £10.

Thus the use of steam power, well, gathered steam. In 1892, Monsieur LeBlanc of Paris, France, ordered the world's first steam-powered motor van for La Belle Jardinière—a high-profile department store that proudly emblazoned it with the message "Livraison à Domicile" (deliveries to home).

But it was still years before trucks of any design strayed far from city limits. Long distances were still dominated by railroads at the turn of the twentieth century. Even where roads were available, the solid rubber wheels and primitive suspensions of early trucks hardly offered a ride that any driver would want to endure for a long period of time.

Still, there were early attempts at longer, more challenging distances. Monsieur Felix Dubois set up a business in 1899 to link the 250-mile route between Kayes and Bamako in the French Sudan. The 9½-hp DeDietrich gasoline-driven trucks that were built to the design of Amedée Bollée of Luneville, France, were expected to suit his needs. Chinese coolies were hired to work the controls. But there were no made-up roads to speak of in the Sudan, and the desert sand quickly choked exposed working parts. The entire business collapsed within a few months.

One of the first long-distance trips of any consequence was in 1911, when a Swiss-built Saurer truck traveled across the United States from Los Angeles, California, to New York, New York. The next year, a Packard truck hauled a three-ton

BELOW The cannon mover built in 1770 by Nicolas Joseph Cugnot. It may have looked rather odd, but it moved without the aid of any animal.

load from New York to San Francisco, California, in 46 days. Even so, such distances remained simple experiments for many years to come.

But if the turn of the century marked the birth of the truck, the vehicle grew to maturity in World War I. The U.S. Society of Automotive Engineers (S.A.E.) had already formed in 1905, looking to develop standards for various automotive components, but its ideas didn't really impact on the trucking industry until the outset of the war. It was then that the S.A.E. was approached by a U.S. military weary of trying to repair different makes of trucks without any set standards for parts. Fifty S.A.E. engineers from a variety of companies gave birth to the standards for the Liberty Class B in the call for a common truck. And by Armistice Day in November 1918, there were 9,364 of the trucks in service. The servicemen who learned to use them in the war returned to North America to build the backbone of a fledgling trucking industry. Europeans found themselves with about 9,000 used trucks that became a staple of civilian trucking throughout the 1920s, after hopeful owner-drivers picked through the hulking metal piles abandoned by Americans in government vehicle dumps. (The Liberty was even used as the basis for Willeme trucks made in France.) Similarly, British manufacturers of the day were influenced by the subvention scheme that gave civilian truck owners an annual cash payment when they promised to make equipment available in times of national emergency. But to be eligible, the vehicles had to conform to specifications involving such things as interchangeable wheels and tires, and bodywork and equipment fittings.

Once it was proven that vehicles could be bought and repaired far away from their factories, the truck truly began to spread its influence. As truck owners became more familiar with the equipment, however, they also forced an increasing focus on vehicle components. While they were close cousins to automobiles, early trucks still faced far greater demands, especially with early users loading chassis well beyond their design limits. With a combination of heavy weights and the rough ride of solid tires, for example, spring leaves were simply collapsing under the stresses of day-to-day work.

Even though Michelin developed pneumatic tires to offer automobiles smoother rides as early as 1912, such tires weren't used on trucks until the 1920s, when casings could withstand the demands of the job. And while these air-filled tires eventually offered smoother rides and limited the stresses on components such as frames, they also brought problems of their own. Giant pneumatics ran under pressures as high as 200 psi and increased frame and body heights. A 1920 three-tonner Packard bought in the U.S.A. needed 44 x 10 pneumatic tires compared to the 36 x 5 solid rubber tires that preceded them. Even so, drivers loved these wheels and their smoother rides. And they loved how truck speeds could increase with them.

Now traveling at speeds as high as 30 miles per hour, however, the trucks were plagued by burnt-out bearings, thrown rods, and engine seizures. Manufacturers actually began building trucks around the tires, with such makers as Packard offering a larger engine for their use.

Even once the higher speeds could be reached with confidence, there were still problems associated with stopping. When drivers attempted to brake through the driveline (or jackshaft of chain-driven units) at speeds of 30 miles per hour, universal

LA SUPÉRIORITÉ INCONTESTÉE
du DIESEL-BERLIET

joints were sheared, differential gears were stripped, and axle shafts broken. It wasn't long before brakes had to evolve.

A major advancement in braking came in the 1920s, when Westinghouse showed that an engine-mounted compressor and a flexible air circuit could provide more stopping power than a foot could produce through a traditional mechanical linkage. The air lines were certainly more flexible than straight linkages, and the advancement even brought brakes to trailers. It's a concept that's still at the heart of modern braking systems.

But not every new idea is quick to gain recognition around the world. Despite the early acceptance of diesel in European trucks, for example, the fuel that now dominates the industry wasn't widely accepted in North America until the 1930s. Diesel may have been cheaper, but there were the annoying sounds of "diesel knock" from the combustion process. Gasoline was the order of the day.

When the world was plunged into World War II, mechanized warfare once again developed to a new level. And once again, advances carried into the peacetime world. Here, for example, were new approaches in detergent oils and lubes, and air filtration developed too. Before the "self-cleaning" oils created during the war became available, truckers had to deal with the sludge and build-up of engine deposits that came with the use of such lubricants as straight mineral oil. (Once the sludge was gone, they had to deal with new-found leaks.) Advances in metallurgy made components both lighter and more durable, playing a particular role in advancing long-haul designs.

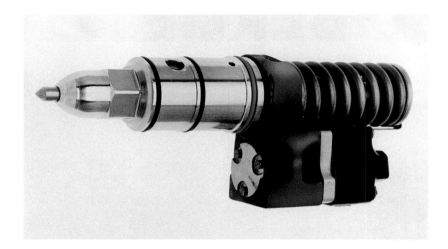

By the 1950s, companies such as Thermo King and Universal were building mechanical refrigeration units for trailers, replacing ice and holdover plates, and making it possible to ship virtually anything by truck. That same decade, the robust worm gear designs that made high-speed linehauls possible in western North America began to give way to advancements in gearing and interaxle differentials. (Although their durability was missed. Even when worn to the limit, a worm could be reversed for a lifetime that extended a few hundred thousand miles.)

But the crises that drive technological advances don't necessarily come in a time of war. The American trucking industry was dealt a shock in late 1973 and early 1974 when an Arab embargo on oil sales sent fuel prices skyrocketing. That forced the industry as a whole to place a greater emphasis on fuel efficiency. At the same time, environmental groups were crying out for cleaner-burning power sources unlike those that powered smoke-belching trucks. Trucks and their engines had to change. Engine air supplies were improved with the introduction of turbocharging, then air-to-air charge air cooling. And the Detroit Diesel Corporation introduced its first

ABOVE The Detroit Diesel Corporation's first electronically controlled fuel injection system. Introduced in 1985, it heralded a new era for the diesel combustion process.

BELOW A 1923 Kenworth model on display. Times change, but each Kenworth truck is a classic.

electronically controlled fuel injection system in 1985, heralding a new era for the diesel combustion process.

Where engine electronics were initially used to control fuel injection, they were later used to gather information concerning engine diagnostics and operating parameters. Truck owners discovered they could even track the habits of their drivers. (Just how often was a particular driver speeding when on the highway?)

The world of satellites came to the trucking industry in 1988, when trucking giant Schneider National installed a Qualcomm unit in a truck to be tracked from the sky. The technology quickly emerged in long-haul trucks throughout the world. Indeed, technology has become a trucker's ever-watchful "Big Brother." Information about a truck is now almost as valuable as the cargo itself. Delivery schedules have embraced a Just-In-Time emphasis that is eliminating the need for traditional warehouse space and allowing manufacturers to look at trucks as warehouses on wheels. So the role of trucks has grown with the trucks themselves.

Developing nations such as China, India, Mexico, and Brazil are looking to the trucking industry to power their emerging economies. And as tools for the job, the trucks of today are being called upon to offer more than ever. They're being asked to do more, perform more efficiently, and last longer than ever. But the challenges will undoubtedly be met—modern engineers have yet to run out of steam.

TRUCKS OF THE WORLD
THE GLOBAL BUSINESS OF TRUCKING

A title of "Trucks of the World" may be more telling than it appears at first glance. In a modern age, the business of making heavy-duty trucks has become a worldwide affair. Leading truck makers may still be based in North America and Europe, with many of their names tracing back to the industry's early days at the turn of the twentieth century, but control of the nameplates is shifting. Daimler-Benz of Stuttgart, Germany, for example, not only controls the Mercedes-Benz label but those of Freightliner and Sterling in North America. The U.S.-based PACCAR organization, which owns Peterbilt and Kenworth, now owns European-based Foden and DAF. Even the trucks themselves are spreading to new frontiers, with an emphasis on emerging markets such as China, India, Russia, and Central and South America. (They can even take on different identities. The Volvo NH Series sold in Australia, for example, is largely a re-badged VN-Series truck from North America.)

But with the worldwide focus comes a sometimes confusing approach to making trucks. In Europe, a technique known as vertical integration sees the makers of trucks manufacturing a variety of drivetrain components. Under the hood of a Mercedes or Scania truck in Europe, for example, you'll probably find a Mercedes or Scania engine—much like what you would expect when purchasing a car. In North America, truck makers tend to avoid the business of making engines. There you find labels such as Caterpillar, Cummins, and Detroit Diesel under the hoods bearing names like Freightliner, Peterbilt, and Kenworth. (Although Volvo and Mack offer proprietary engines and drivetrains in North America, their businesses are still dominated by

BELOW Under the hood of long-nose truck in North America, you're not likely to find a proprietary engine.

other component makers.) And when European truck makers take their designs to the tough-trucking terrain of Australia, they're typically married to the more robust components made in North America, such as the transmissions built by Meritor (formerly known as Rockwell Automotive) and Eaton. Even Canadian trucks differ from their U.S. counterparts with robust additions such as frame inserts and heavier frame rails. Yet these trucks increasingly travel the same highways with a growing focus on north-south trade routes. If you don't think these issues are confusing enough, consider that several European manufacturers are looking to include an array of engines from other sources, such as those made by Caterpillar, Cummins, and Detroit Diesel; and Freightliner officials have brought a Mercedes engine to North America. Within each of the dozens of engine designs that are on the market today is a wide array of power ranges. That's why this book's profiles of engines have been limited to the most powerful designs available, and are listed independently of details about the trucks themselves. You never know where they will appear in the future.

It would be impossible to list every truck option or every truck line for that matter, given that each truck is customized to the needs of its owner, to the needs of the job at hand. But the following pages offer looks at the long-haul trucks that ply today's highways, with a particular focus on the designs of their cabs and exteriors, and a nod to the history of their makers.

Each market has its own needs, its own operating environment, and its own regulations telling how much can be hauled—and an economy that will determine if parts are available to keep them rolling. But whatever badge they carry, the long-haul trucks of the world continue to fascinate even those who simply pass them on the highway. They are, after all, the undisputed kings of the road.

DAF TRUCKS N.V.
THE NETHERLANDS

You could say that brothers Hub and Wim Van Doorne entered the trucking industry through the back door, manufacturing semi-trailers along with ladders, metal cabinets, and window frames in 1928. But in 1936 they ventured into the business of powered vehicles with Trado all-wheel-drive conversion kits for Fords and other trucks used by the Dutch Army. And in 1938 they manufactured their first complete vehicle in a 6 x 4 armored car.

Their first truck came in 1950—two years after the company's first bus—as a five-ton forward-control conventional model powered by a six-cylinder Hercules gasoline engine and other proprietary components. The final design boasted four forward speeds, hydrovac brakes, and the option of diesel power with a 4.7-liter Perkins engine.

Today's DAF carries a line of both medium- and heavy-duty trucks built at its factories in The Netherlands and Belgium, and sells lightweight Leyland trucks in Continental Europe. But it also carries a foreign flair.

The company was sold to North American-based PACCAR in November 1996.

BELOW DAF's 95XF is the flagship of a modern truck line with a worldwide flair. The company was sold to PACCAR in 1996.

THE 95XF
A TRUCK FOR THE SPACE AGE

DAF wanted "Felix III" to feel comfortable in the 95XF. As well he should.

The truck maker built its long-haul truck line around this stereotypical driver, expected to sit behind the wheel between 2005 and 2010. And it was a case of covering extremes, from 65- to 76¾-inch heights. In the midst of it all, the cab had to be comfortable for the average driver who stretches 6 feet from head to toe.

In many respects, the 95XF looks much like its predecessor, the DAF 95, except for new doors and a distinctive black grille. But it's such things as the wide-open spaces inside the cab that set this truck apart.

The air-suspended driver's seat, developed by Isringhausen, floats back and forth through a seven-inch range, raising or lowering 3.9 inches. The compact 17.7-inch steering wheel can be tilted 35 to 45 degrees, and lifted or lowered through a 3.3-inch range. (Pressing a button on the steering column allows the wheel's position to be changed. If the wheel is not locked in place within seven seconds, it does so on its own.)

As a whole, all XF cabs are 3.9 inches longer than the original DAF 95. The U.K.-devoted Comfort Cab and its normal roof (62½ inches), Space Cab with its high roof (74½ inches) and Super Space Cab with the tallest roof yet (88½ inches) all offer a 88½-inch-long cab that makes room for Europe's largest moving bed. The 31.8 x 80.7 x 6-inch Lastilux mattress is so wide that it's sculpted to make room for the driver and passenger seats.

An upper bunk in the Comfort Cab and Space Cab measures 77 x 23½ inches, while in the Super Space Cab it's 75½ x 27½ inches. And the 98-inch-wide cab itself is so deep that the bunk can remain in the sleeping position while the truck moves down the road. Such comfort is becoming more of an issue in Europe as eastern borders open ever wider and long-haul trips become more of a way of life.

ABOVE The grille design of the 95XF helps differentiate it from its predecessor, the DAF 95.

MANUFACTURER: DAF Trucks N.V.

TRUCK: 95XF

DISTINCTIVE FEATURES: Interior designed around extensive study of ergonomics.

PREMIUM SLEEPER: Super Space Cab

For life on a long haul, storage is crucial. The Super Space Cab includes 21 dedicated storage departments, eight of which are enclosed and illuminated. Lockers above the six-degree windshield offer 26,835 cubic inches of room. With compartments against the lower sides of the cab, above the doors, and under the lower bunk, there's a total of 65,880 cubic inches of storage space. Lockers above the windshield in the Space Cab offer 10,370 cubic inches of storage and, as is the case with its larger cousin, the middle locker is large enough to accommodate a microwave and coffee maker. (Overall, the Space Cab offers 50,630 cubic inches of storage space.) Outside, a sealed, lockable compartment is available for wet gear and tools. Inside there are large storage areas under the bed.

More comfort is found in an attention to details: the radio is placed on an angled fascia just left of the driver. And the slide-out table found in the old 95 now extends back far enough so that a driver can use it while sitting on the bunk.

Improved cab insulation has reduced in-cab noise to 66 decibels when the truck is traveling at 52 miles per hour—and that's less noise than that enjoyed by most luxury cars. A four-point cab suspension with rear horizontal dampers improves the ride quality felt in the seat of the driver's pants, while a four-point air suspension is standard on the Super Space Cab. The XF has 70.8-inch parabolic springs at the front and the four-bag ECAS electronically controlled air suspension at the rear.

It's a truck built to last 25 percent longer than its predecessor—built to go the distance and cut costs: a complete airflow management kit consists of a roof spoiler, side deflectors, side skirts, corner spoilers, and an air dam. Even longer doors also play a role in aerodynamics, by overlapping the upper steps.

For the fuel that is burned, pressed steel fuel tanks are standard, while aluminum is optional. Apart from 105- or 158-gallon tanks, the 95XF can also be ordered with a storage tank holding 198 or 238 gallons of fuel, sufficient for ranges of 1,550 to 1,864 miles. Combinations of 158 and 79 gallons, or 158 and 105 gallons are also available.

Powering the trip is a new 24-valve, 12.6-liter power unit. The turbocharged and intercooled in-line engine offers 16 percent more tractive effort coupled with four percent lower fuel consumption. And for those with a thirst for power, a Cummins six-cylinder, 14-liter, in-line engine is available with a rating of 530 hp.

For stopping power, the 95XF is fitted with high-performance air pressure drum brakes. Brake shoes have a 30 percent better life than pads, and drums will last some 65 percent longer than discs prevalent on other European designs.

The SR 1347 single-reduction rear axle is one of the NAG (New Axle Generation) variety, incorporating two parts from flat sheet steel. The final result is rated at 13 tons, yet is 0.88 hundredweight lighter than previous hypoid-type axles. A high-grade rear axle is available in ratios varying from 2.93:1 to 4.10:1

Heavy applications, meanwhile, can take advantage of the DAF HR 1354 rear axle with hub reduction. Low Deck variants with small wheels, and a gearbox with overdrive on the top gear are among several available options.

Normal loads and normal roads require the medium-duty M chassis with a 10.2-inch-high side member, with no inside stiffeners. In heavier applications with high axle loads and high local loading of the chassis on poor roads, the H chassis fills the bill. It has 12.2-inch-high side members for rigids and 10.2-inch-high side members for tractors, with the chassis considered standard for 8- and 8.5-ton front axles.

COUNTER CLOCKWISE FROM TOP LEFT Robust frame rails; interior storage options; a massive moving bed; maintenance access; under-bunk storage; a fully adjustable steering wheel; storage in the header; an intercooled in-line engine help set the 95XF apart from its predecessors.

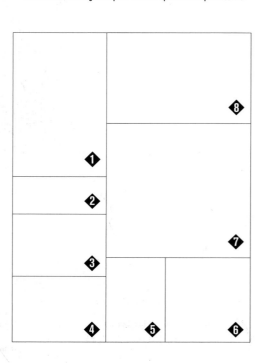

DAIMLER-BENZ AG
GERMANY

It's ironic, really, that Gottlieb Daimler and Karl Benz hardly knew each other. As they struggled with early engine designs in the 1880s, their workshops were a mere 60 miles apart in Germany's Neckar Valley. More remarkable still is that they took separate paths toward the same goal of designing practical engines. Benz began working on two-stroke engine designs while Daimler was working for Nikolaus August Otto, who had already established four-stroke engines as the industry's standard. But Benz's 1882 patent for a two-stroke engine had merit—particularly in its form of control that was a pioneer in gas-throttle designs. He didn't begin building four-stroke engines until 1885, after Otto lost the associated patent in a lawsuit.

Benz built his first vehicle in 1885: a three-wheeled design powered by an exposed four-stroke engine capable of $2/3$ horsepower at 250 to 300 rpm, moving at a top speed of 9.9 miles per hour. Daimler followed with his first automobile later in 1886. Although their businesses weren't merged until 1926, the resulting company would become one of the world's most recognized makers of luxury cars and commercial trucks. (Daimler never saw the day. He died in 1900.)

Early Daimler-Benz truck designs weren't much to look at, but the detail found in their engines attracted a great deal of attention. The most popular feature of Mercedes-Benz trucks in the late 1920s was their six-cylinder, 8.5-liter engines that generated 75 hp. The company continues to make its own engines.

Without a doubt, Daimler-Benz and its commercial vehicle units, including Mercedes-Benz, Freightliner, and Sterling, dominate the world of truck making. Its commercial vehicle division alone employs more than 85,000 people, selling 417,384 commercial vehicles in 1997 from Africa to Asia, and from Germany to North America.

Perhaps the three-pointed star identifying the Mercedes brand is appropriate, for it truly is a star in the business.

BELOW Daimler-Benz sold 417,384 commercial vehicles in 1997, with designs including the Actros.

THE ACTROS
NEW TO THE LAST BOLT

It's a very bold statement indeed to refer to a truck line as the world's most advanced range of heavy trucks, but that's exactly what Mercedes-Benz claims with the Actros. The truck was unveiled as a design that was new down to the last chassis bolt. That means new cabs and new engines when compared to the 23-year-old SK range that it replaced in 1997 (although, the older range had seen extensive changes over the course of the years).

Actros cabs come from a new "Body in White 2000" cab production system—a modular approach that leads to the offering of a standard sleeper, high-roof sleeper, premium day cab, and the top-of-the-line MegaSpace cab. With a uniform exterior width of 98 inches, they are available in lengths of 46, 76, and 86½ inches, with an interior width of 88 inches. A standard height in the S, M and L cabs reaches up to 61 inches, while there's a hi-roof version that's 75 inches high.

For under the hood there are seven available power ratings that range from 313 to 571 hp, and about 880 pounds is trimmed from the truck's overall weight when compared to previous designs. A front axle that's set back 29.9 inches sits under the truck with a wheelbase of 141.7 or 153½ inches. (The Actros' turning circle ranges from 49 to 51½ feet.) And the overall length ranges between 228 and 240 inches.

The exterior shaping of the truck's lines has reduced wind resistance by 17 percent when compared to previous models. And there are the potential additions of three adjustable roof spoilers, matching cab extenders in two lengths for semi-trailer tractors, lateral fairings for the different wheelbases, and covers for the front and

ABOVE Actros models—unveiled as the world's most advanced trucks—replaced the 23-year-old SK range.

MANUFACTURER: Mercedes-Benz

TRUCK: Actros

DISTINCTIVE FEATURES: Modular cab design with offerings from a premium day cab to the top-of-the-line Mega Space Cab

PREMIUM SLEEPER: Mega Space Cab

rear wheels. Overall, there's the opportunity to improve aerodynamics by another 4.5 to 14.5 percent, depending on the model of truck.

Much to the delight of traffic that shares the road with the Actros, profiled linings on the insides of wheel arches fling water to the center of the truck to minimize road spray. For the sake of further safety, lateral and rear underride guards have been improved, and there's an optional front underride guard. All of them can withstand an impact of 17.6 tons.

For engine access, the cab tilts 70 degrees. And when the driver needs to access the inside of the cab, Actros doors open 95 degrees, with three steps heading into most models (the MegaSpace needing four steps).

Once inside, there's the view through a massive 12-degree windshield. Two wiper arms that incorporate windshield washer nozzles can be controlled with intermittent wiper settings of between two and 20 seconds. And with the dirt-diverting profile of the A-Pillars and heated rearview mirrors, the view from the Actros is yet further enhanced.

But each of the Actros cabs also boasts its own set of features. The Standard Sleeper L Cab is designed primarily for fleets, with 4 x 2 and 6 x 2 configurations fitted with a 354-hp V6 engine that can cruise at 56 mph at 1,436 rpm.

The low-height V6 engine means a lower doghouse, while storage space includes areas to store tachometer discs, notebooks, pens, and a mobile phone. Seats are trimmed in velour, while the floor is covered with rubber, with carpet draped over the engine tunnel. To help keep out the sun, a lateral sun visor is offered on the driver's side, while 180-degree curtains offer privacy for the sleeper. And a night heater creates a cozy atmosphere when required.

For longer distances, however, there's the high-roof model that can be fitted with both V6 and V8 engines. The L-type roof sleeper offers a single bunk, but there are other comforts to be had. The driver's window is electric, two roller sunblinds help keep out the sun, and an electric sunroof will let it in. Front fog lamps help light the way, while a lockable battery cover is accented by a 132-gallon alloy fuel tank.

With its level floor, the MegaSpace cab has an interior standing height of 75 inches.

LEFT Daimler-Benz remains committed to building its own engine designs as other truck makers outsource the work.

It's also available with a special streamlining package for a design that is 145 inches high—10½ inches higher than the L cab.

For the true professional, however, there's the executive model. Offered as a truck "to cross not just countries, but continents," this truck is built to accommodate its 16 liters of engine with 530/571 hp and 1,770 lb-ft/1,992 lb-ft of torque, all controlled by the Mercedes 16-speed Telligent shifter. Inside, the flat-floor, high-datum MegaSpace cab offers twin bunks with a fully carpeted floor and engine tunnel. Additional storage is available above the windshield, while two 12-volt sockets offer power for the amenities of home with the help of a 100-amp alternator. Front driving lamps light the way for the truck that rolls on aluminum wheels with a 155-gallon alloy fuel tank.

The driver's suspension seat can travel 7¾ inches, and lifts just under 4 inches, with the seat squab angle adjustable through 17 degrees; the backrest through six degrees forward and 36 degrees back. The 17¾-inch diameter steering wheel can be

ABOVE Views from the cab are enhanced by everything from dirt-diverting A pillars to wiper arms that incorporate washer nozzles.

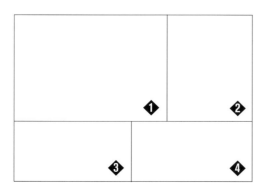

ABOVE It's an attention to detail that helps set the Actros apart. The low-height V6 engine means a lower doghouse 1, the truck's doors act as safety struts in the event of an accident 2, the width of the bunk can be extended 3, and there is an expansive area under the lower bunk for extra storage 4.

adjusted through a range of 2½ inches and an angle of between 20 and 33 degrees.

Safety systems include an air bag, and belt tensioners that are integrated into the seats. Even the floor assembly and seat base were designed to absorb forces of up to 95 g—40 times the normal g force—while the doors will act as safety struts to improve survival space in the event of an accident.

In the angled cowling at the right of the driver in an executive cab is an integrated instrument cluster with a flat tachograph and automatic disc insertion, a large rev counter, gear display, and a centrally located Stop warning light with two liquid crystal displays. The center section of the instrument panel extends slightly into the cab with rotary switches for heating, ventilation, and air conditioning, and three rows of rocker switches. Below the switch panel is an ashtray and cigarette lighter behind a flap, with a lockable radio recess next to it. Even the co-driver gets an ashtray and cigarette lighter. A lockable box above the windshield is for such things as a CB, while a storage tray on the engine tunnel includes such controls as the parking brake valve and roof light switches, as well as holders for 5¼-pint PET bottles, cups or cans, and a removable litter bin.

The top-of-the-range radio unit—the Sound 6024—can be wired in with an infrared remote control and a CD player. Speakers are fitted in the outer corners on the shelf above the windshield, with optional stereo loudspeakers fitted in the left-hand corner and center, as well as in the center and right-hand corner to allow team drivers to enjoy stereo sound.

The cowling in front of the co-driver holds a second storage tray, while the covered electric compartment stores fuses, electric modules, sockets, and the connector for an external diagnostic system. Two openings for ventilation have been moved to the upper portion of the rear wall, with fresh air drawn in from a dust-free point behind the front flap and cleaned by a standard particle filter (although an activated charcoal filter is available to reduce odors).

The bunks are 77 inches long and 23½ inches wide, but can be extended to widths of 29½ inches. And the three folding sections of the lower bunk make it easier to access storage compartments without having to clear the entire bunk. The control panel behind the lower bunk offers controls for auxiliary heating, the sunroof and blind, as well as a built-in alarm clock. A second upper bunk available in the Long Distance and MegaSpace cabs is undivided but can also be expanded to the 29½-inch width. Without the bunk, though, there's room for a wall-mounted cabinet with storage, a refrigerator, a microwave oven, and a coffee machine.

Outside of the Actros, nothing protrudes beyond the upper edge of the frame, which is available in $^{17}/_{64}$-, $^{5}/_{16}$-, and $^{3}/_{8}$-inch widths, with a uniform web height of 10½ inches.

The four cabs come with a choice of several suspension designs. The S and M front cab suspension systems include a rubber-cushioned tilt mounting with shock absorbers fitted on the outside. To the rear, they are mounted on spring struts. But for the L and MegaSpace cabs, four-point mountings with shock-absorbing spring

ABOVE But the details don't stop there. Seatbelts are integrated into the seats 2, computers keep an eye on engine diagnostics 3, electronic shifting means an end to traditional shift levers 4, there's a driver's side air bag 5, and all of it sits in a cab that will tilt 70 degrees to provide engine access 6.

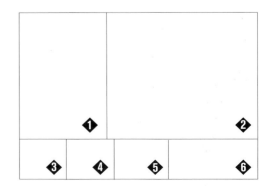

struts and a front stabilizer were also developed. For long-distance cabs, an air suspension incorporates shock absorbers with four mounting points and a front stabilizer. On the twin-axle units of the three-axle vehicles, the swing axle suspension is replaced by parabolic springs, reducing the number of layers and the system's weight. Tapered roller bearings were replaced by maintenance-free rubber molecular bearings with spring ends located in non-wearing rubber pressure elements. The twin-axle units are located by triangular links that ensure more precise axle location and are not subject to transverse forces, resulting in reduced wear, and permitting maintenance-free mountings.

When it's time to stop, there's the Telligent brake-by-wire system with disc brakes that will halt an Actros traveling at 53 miles per hour a full 59 feet sooner than a conventional braking system. Indeed, EBS (the electronic braking system) also offers better overall stability during severe braking events. And the monitored system leads to the added benefit of uniform disc pad wear. The pressure of the air reservoir was raised to 10 bar (previously 8.5 bar) for quicker response. New components, such as valves and pressure lines, make the higher pressures possible in the first place. And the 22½-inch internally ventilated disc brakes are fitted on all wheels.

The brake control unit adjusts brake performance in accordance with weights. A certain brake pedal travel always generates the same level of deceleration—no matter how heavily laden the truck may be. When engine brakes are specified, they're incorporated into the overall brake system, cutting back the retarder function in stages or switching it off completely before the ABS cuts in.

The distribution of axle loads is calculated on the basis of the difference between front and rear axle wheel speeds. Gradients are taken into account in the calculations as well as the activation of the retarder or decompression valve engine brake. As a result, the system doesn't need a load sensor to "know" how heavily the vehicle is laden and how the load is distributed between the axles, processing the slip values when the vehicle first starts. After a few brakings, the system can tell whether the trailer brakes contribute to the overall combination's deceleration in accordance with the trailer load. Control pressure to the trailer continues to be transmitted through the trailer brake coupling point. That means the system is also capable of controlling brakes on older trailers. If the trailer brakes do not adequately contribute to the truck's stopping power, the control pressure

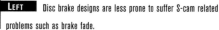

LEFT Disc brake designs are less prone to suffer S-cam related problems such as brake fade.

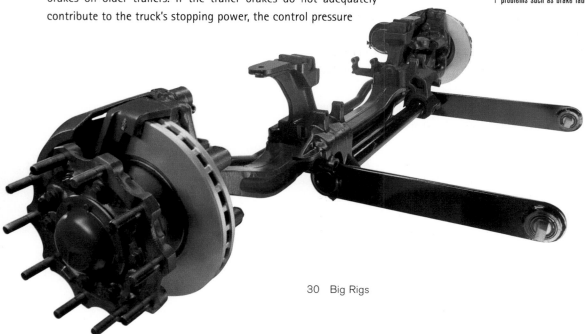

fed through the coupling point is corrected. The wheel hubs are fitted with rotors for recording wheel speeds, with the signals processed by the ABS and ASR (Anti-Skid) control units and passed on through the CAN databus. The ASR technology is also a standard feature. And it's with the help of such sensors that pre-trip inspections mean looking at the tires and the cleanliness of the windshield, windows, and mirrors, with the on-board computer offering the rest of the information, displaying warnings for servicing work in plain language.

There's also the choice of two electronic transmissions. Building on the EPS system introduced in 1986, they maximize the effectiveness of the powertrain with faster and smoother gear changes. While the driver is operating the clutch and the gear selection lever, he is not physically changing the gear himself. Once the clutch is operated by the driver, the compressed-air cylinders and solenoid valves change gears, while the haptic feedback signals the driver to release the clutch pedal again. The Telligent automatic gearshift takes that a step further by even operating the clutch, and the joystick has a switch for splitting gears fitted at the front base. The truck may not quite drive itself, but it does take over a large share of the work.

ABOVE With its Telligent brake-by-wire system, an Actros traveling at 53 mph can stop 59 feet sooner than a truck with conventional brakes.

ERF LTD
ENGLAND

When the era of British-owned heavy truck makers came to an end in 1996, its sunset was at Sun Works. ERF Ltd had remained true to its British roots that traced back to E.R. Foden, but it was ultimately sold to Canadian-based Western Star so that it could remain competitive.

Foden gave his name to the firm that built diesel-powered trucks as early as 1933, only a mile from the Foden family factory that was a pioneer in steam power. He had retired from the family business in 1931 after a fight over company strategy, but was persuaded by his son Dennis to build trucks with proprietary diesel engines and components—not forgetting an ERF nameplate. (The original Foden firm is still located a mile away from Sun Works, although it too has North American owners.)

The first ERF-badged design was built in the corner of the J.H. Jennings and Son coach-making facility, close to the town center of Sandbach. And a new factory that was built on an adjacent plot of land in 1939 remains part of the present-day company headquarters.

ERF was the first truck builder in Britain to use the standard "fail-safe" spring brakes that offer parking brakes on every axle; it was a pioneer in the use of glass-reinforced plastic in cab construction; and it introduced electronic engine controls in 1996 with the EC range of trucks. Today, it looks to the mainland of the European Union for a chance to grow.

THE EC
AN OLYMPIC-CALIBER TRUCK

With its high-end options carrying an Olympic label, you'd expect ERF's EC Cab to be a winner. And indeed, the top of the truck line incorporates a chassis streamlining kit, vertical exhaust, and Connolly leather seating for a distinct look from other ECs. But every EC Cab shares a series of attributes.

The cabs are built with panels created from a sheet-molded compound (SMC), which in turn are mounted to multicoated steel subframes with corrosion-resistant fittings. And by working with SMC, designers didn't have to worry about the panels bending or rusting, and were able to give the cab a 10-year warranty. (It also meets Europe's stringent crash-worthiness criteria.)

Drivers can step through the doors that open 90 degrees thanks to the help of three equally spaced steps and grab handles. Inside, the cab—that can be fitted with right- or left-hand drive—incorporates a deep windshield, large side windows, and a low, heated mirror for its view of the outside world. The fascia at the front of the cab has not only been designed for better forward visibility, but offers room for easier access to the cab. And the EC's ride is balanced with a four-point cab suspension.

The passenger seat can swivel 360 degrees to offer additional seating in the sleeper, while the top bunk will fold away for added room. A built-in clothes closet, overhead lockers, and external locker all add to the all-important storage space in a home away from home.

An electronically controlled heating system, with an optional integral air conditioner, offers infinitely variable fan speeds, will filter pollen, and will blow fresh

MANUFACTURER: ERF Ltd

TRUCK: EC

DISTINCTIVE FEATURES: Sheet-molded compound cab mounted to multi-coated steel subframes with corrosion resistant fittings

PREMIUM SLEEPER: Olympic

BELOW Every EC cab is built using sheet-molded compound (SMC). This does not bend or rust, and allows the cab to have a 10-year warranty.

air on the faces of both driver and passenger. A high-performance night heater, meanwhile, is offered with an indicator that warns the driver about low external air temperatures.

Transmission options include the eight-, nine-, 12-, and 16-speed synchromesh designs from Eaton and ZF; a 12-speed twin splitter from Eaton; and nine- or 13-speed range charge transmissions from Eaton that incorporate four PTO positions. All models are fitted with a twin plate ceramic-faced clutch, with a seven-spring soft center and keystone-ground ceramic facings that incorporate a positive plate separator for smoother operation, working to improve the life of the driveline.

Nothing protrudes above the chassis' frame rails, to allow better compatibility to trailers, while standard positions will fit pumping and hydraulic gears, and there's a standard autolube system. An optional ERF integrated catwalk is also available.

Underneath, the front suspension uses taperleaf springs with long stroke dampers and an antiroll bar for maximum stability. Although two- or four-bellow air systems are also available, the ERF two-bellow nonreactive system delivers the ride of a four-bellow model but with the weight and lower cost that comes with two. Rubber suspensions will maintain traction whatever the terrain.

Weight-saving options include a lightweight braking system, alloy fuel tank, alloy wheels, and small-diameter wheels and tires.

ERF road-ready kits are fitted with fixed or sliding fifth wheels and lead-up ramps, and include two-line hoses and couplings, the ERF catwalk, trailer hook-up, lamp, black plastic wings, and mudflaps on the drive axle.

Fixed and adjustable aerodynamic systems are fitted with fixed or hinged side skirts. Headlamp wash wipe and twin fog and spot lamps can be found outside with a full range of steel and alloy, single or twin fuel tanks.

An optional immobilizer and/or alarm system meeting THATCHAM requirements can foil thieves, automatically arming itself in high-risk urban areas where the driver often leaves the cab. It can be combined with an optional central locking system.

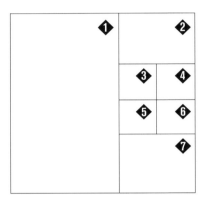

RIGHT The cab has many special features. Clockwise from upper right: the fascia at the front of the cab has been designed for better visibility and offers room for easier access to the cab; storage compartments range from a wardrobe to overhead lockers, while the passenger seat will face the bunk to enhance space in the sleeper; the roof of the cab is designed with aerodynamics in mind. Options range from hinged side skirts to the contoured roof line.

❶		❷
	❸	❹
	❺	❻
		❼

LEFT Entry into the EC cab is eased with three equally-spaced steps and doors that open 90 degrees.

1

2

WESTERN STAR: THE COMMANDER
THE ERF WITH AN AUSTRALIAN BADGE

Although ERF's EC cabs are shipped to Australia, they are enhanced with a variety of options meant to make them suitable for the B-double business common to the massive island nation—specifically to allow the loading of 34 pallets over two trailers in an 82-foot combination length.

The front axle is repositioned to allow the maximum legal weight payload on all axles, offering up to 2.2 tons of additional payload when compared to that of other cabover trucks in the Australian market, says Western Star.

To meet the demanding needs of a rugged terrain, the truck is coupled with Cummins N14 engines rated from 430 to 525 hp in 6 x 4 and 8 x 4 ratings, as well as with Series 60 Detroit Diesel engines. A Fuller RTLO18718 transmission is added along with other North American components including the Rockwell RT46-160P rear axles together with a Hendrickson HAS461 rear air suspension which allows payloads of up to 99 tons.

A twin-steer, four-axle 8 x 4 version is designed for Western Australia and New Zealand. The 6 x 4 can be distinguished from its 8 x 4 brethren from a head-on view, with its four seven-inch headlamps and round indicator lamps set in a colored front bumper. The 8 x 4, meanwhile, has two rectangular lamps and rectangular indicators.

The models are designated 7564F and 7564S respectively, indicating forward-mounted or setback axles for B-double or traditional semitrailer applications. An optional B-doubles package includes Meritor-Wabco antilock brakes with autoslack adjusters, heavy-duty plastic mudguards, and a spray suppression kit.

The all-steel chassis for the Australian trucks matches the 34-inch width common in North America, to make for a better fit with the rear axle and suspension components. The 10.7 x 3.6 x 0.3-inch chassis rails are made with a 110,000-psi heat-treated steel alloy that's used on other Western Star trucks.

The cabin is mounted on coil springs and dampers at four points, the rear two of which can be raised or lowered individually. It claims to be the quietest-running cabover truck in Australia, with the help of the SMC cab and an inch of glass fiber matting to baffle the sounds on the engine sides. The engine itself has a steel frame cover with a half inch of insulation to protect drivers from high-frequency noise, and

MANUFACTURER:	Western Star
TRUCK:	Commander
DISTINCTIVE FEATURES:	ERF cab design

BELOW Options make the design suitable for B-double business.

$3/32$ inch of high density PVC insulation offers protection against low-frequency noise. The mounting of the gear lever has been sound-proofed, and noise is further baffled with $1/10$ inch of carpet.

Daily maintenance checks are made easier without the need to tilt the cab to look at coolant, engine oil, and clutch or brake fluid levels. Although, when it's time for heavier work, the hydraulic 60-degree tilt-locking cab operates automatically from a cab tilt pump, eliminating the need to operate separate cab locks.

Dual air intakes set high at the rear of the cab are beyond the spray of the front wheels, with dual Cyclopac air filters ensuring that the dust stays out. The truck is further protected with a stone guard for the windshield and an exterior sun visor to offer protection from the elements, while trim panels are finished with traditional Western Star woodgrain inserts on the dash and doors. It may be an ERF, but it carries the Western Star name, after all.

FODEN TRUCKS
ENGLAND

BELOW As a day cab, the 4000 shown here is ideal for bulk hauling.

Edwin Foden was only a year old when the first steam locomotive pulled past his hometown near Sandbach, Cheshire, in 1842. So it's only fitting that he would grow up to study and design engines powered by steam. The entire town had been captivated by the engineering miracle that traveled through their community. Perhaps Foden should thank George Hancock for a start in the trucking business. Hancock began making agricultural parts and steam engines in 1848 at a shop that was only a short distance from the Sandbach station, and Foden joined him as an apprentice in 1856. A decade later, Foden was a partner in the business that had evolved to make portable steam engines for prime movers.

Such engineering was no easy task in that era, particularly with a government that bent to the will of the railroads. An Act of Parliament introduced in 1861, for example, required a man with a red flag to precede all such vehicles; four years later another Act limited road locomotives to moving on turnpike roads between midnight and 6 a.m. The latter meant any firm without a private road wasn't able to test its inventions.

But the engineering did advance and in 1880 Foden improved on traditional one-cylinder steam-powered designs with a compound model that ran at a pressure of 250 pounds while consuming fuel at a rate of 1.86 pounds per horsepower hour.

In 1887, with the help of several backers, Edwin Foden Sons and Co. Ltd was formed and would continue for years as a pioneer in the world of steam-powered wagons. By 1929, though, the company began to consider a future in diesel engines when designs such as those of Mercedes-Benz and Saurer found their way into the British marketplace.

Although it was never a huge company, Foden had its share of engineering success stories. At the 1956 Commercial Motor Show, for example, a Foden with air brakes and power steering was hailed as the "pacemaker for the next five years." Two years later the company was creating reinforced plastic cabs, and in 1964 it introduced the first tilt cab in the British market.

The company may have been sold to U.S.-based PACCAR in 1980, but its history in Britain has yet to show signs of running out of steam.

THE ALPHA RANGE

KITE RIGHT

It's difficult to ignore the similarities of Foden's Alpha Range of trucks and that of the 75- and 85-series of trucks built by its brethren at DAF. The trucks are, after all, built with the same cabs. But the differences go beyond the famous kite on the grille. While the DAF side panels and doors incorporate a flared profile that sweeps toward the wheel well, the Alpha trucks can be identified with their flat sides and stamped door panels.

The Alpha design is available in a range of trucks from 4 x 2 rigids to 6 x 2 and 6 x 4 configurations ranging from 17 to 44 tons, in a choice of seven narrow, full-width, and high-roof models. At the top of the line is the 4000 series, measuring 100 inches wide and available in daycab or sleeper versions with standard-height or Hi-Line high-roof designs. (Sleepers add only 198 pounds to the tare weight of the daycab.) Long-haul operators looking to improve fuel economy have the additional

ABOVE The 3000 series in Foden's Alpha range is for more cost-conscious buyers. For those who want the top of the line, there's the 4000 series.

MANUFACTURER: Foden

TRUCK: The Alpha 4000 Series

BBC: 87.7 inches

DISTINCTIVE FEATURES: Flat sides and stamped door panels distinguish it from DAF models

PREMIUM SLEEPER: 4000 XL

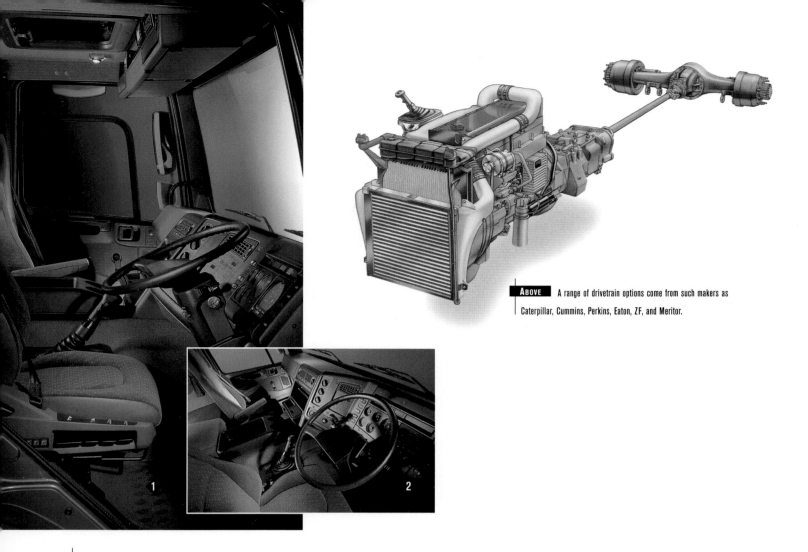

ABOVE Storage options can be found throughout the interior of the Alpha cab, including areas in the dash, on the engine cover and under the seat.

BELOW Frame options include a wraparound steel bumper, with other options including fog lights and spotlights.

option of enhancing aerodynamics with fitted spoilers for the roof and sides.

Looking forward from the driver's seat, the DAF and Foden designs look remarkably similar again except for the badge on the steering wheel. But this is also supposed to be Foden's quietest-ever cab, built of steel and composite GRP construction with aluminum doors, in a design that both meets the standards of European cash criteria and withstands corrosion.

With its "Advanced Function Concept," Foden matches the range of trucks to an array of components—engines from Caterpillar, Cummins, and Perkins with ratings of 275 to 500 bhp; transmissions from Eaton and ZF; and axles from Meritor, for example. The trucks are built on high-tensile steel siderails complete with forged aluminum gusseted crossmembers and an easy-to-maintain bolted construction. And the chassis itself is painted at the factory.

Rides are eased with suspension options ranging from steel springs to Air-Trac full air suspensions and Foden FF20 rubber suspensions.

For those looking to add to the truck, line-fitted options include aluminum wheels and air and fuel tanks; an exhaust brake; chassis lubrication; stainless-steel exhausts; forward or vertical rear exhausts; fire screening; and more. Frame options include a wraparound steel bumper, with other options including fog lights, spotlights, and a clothes closet behind the driver's seat.

While the cab will tilt 65 degrees for maintenance, daily fluid checks can be conducted by opening a hinged front grille.

Inside, storage areas can be found in the dash, on the engine cover, under the seat, in door pockets, and on the rear panel of the cab, with a 9½-inch-deep lockable storage locker under the bunk. And the roof vent found overhead can be opened to one of six positions. Foden hasn't forsaken its customizing heritage.

THE 4000 XL
THE TEAM PLAYER

BELOW The 4000XL cab offers drivers more space than any other Foden design.

When a driving team looks for comfort in a Foden design, it looks up to the 4000 XL double bunk sleeper cab. And while it's designed for team driving, attention has been given to the comfort of each individual. For example, even when the upper bunk is lowered in the sleeping position, there's still room to sit in the lower bunk. And there's 74 inches of room over the engine compartment even when the bunks are in their sleeping positions, offering a more comfortable space to change. Fresh air can be let into the sleeper through an electric sunroof, while an integrated blind can shut

out the sun when it's time to sleep. The colored fascia incorporates walnut trim, while velour-trimmed seats offer a premium touch. A flexible reading lamp is fitted into the electric control panel found on the passenger side of the cab. Instruments are within easy reach of the color coordinated wraparound dashboard. Master control panels located on both the driver and passenger sides of the cab offer full control over such things as the radio and overhead lights. And the console that holds the gearshift also incorporates rocker switches and a holder for drinks cans. The CB/radio-telephone center is located just to the left of the driver.

Storage is further enhanced with space under the bunk, while the bunk face itself offers space to store a vacuum flask or bottle. And aircraft-style lockers above the windshield incorporate nets to keep contents in place once the doors are opened, while side storage areas also incorporate securing nets.

ABOVE With its "Advanced Function Concept," Foden matches the range of trucks to an array of components—engines such as Caterpillar, Cummins and Perkins with ratings of 275 to 500 bhp; transmissions from Eaton and ZF; and axles from Meritor.

FREIGHTLINER CORP
PORTLAND, OREGON, U.S.A.

Leyland James' first experience in truck making came in 1913 when he converted a Packard to deliver sand and gravel. Little did he know that he would revisit the experience more than a quarter century later.

James formed Consolidated Truck Lines in 1929 with a focus on long hauls. But while he rebuilt the Packard to suit the requirements of his first business, he couldn't find a truck maker to fulfill the needs of the Consolidated operation. He wanted a lightweight truck for heavy-duty work that could handle maximum payloads, but nobody was willing to build it. Consolidated mechanics were simply left to find new ways to lighten existing trucks. The answer came in 1939 with a truck of his own.

James formed Freightways Inc. and created the first Freightliner—a Model CF-100 COE design with a diesel engine. A new truck plant was built in Portland, Oregon, in 1947 under a relaunched Freightliner Corporation. (The change in Freightways came about after a U.S. Justice Department suit accused the company of being a monopoly.) And by incorporating an extensive use of aluminum and magnesium, his new trucks were about a ton lighter than already established brands.

The Model 800 "bubble nose"—the first truck to be sold outside the company—was built in 1947. The first sleeper was added two years later. From 1951 to 1977, until the marketing agreement ended, the White Motor Company sold and serviced the trucks with a White Freightliner nameplate.

Freightliner was bought by automotive giant Daimler-Benz in 1981 and today is one of the biggest truck builders in the world, leading sales throughout North America and stretching into markets from South America to China. Its holdings now include Sterling Truck Corporation and American LaFrance.

BELOW The future of North America's largest truck manufacturer—now owned by Daimler Benz—can be seen in the Century Class conventional and the Argosy cabover. It's been generations since Freightliner sold its first Model 800 "bubble nose" tractor in 1947, but the manufacturer is still true to an extensive use of aluminum.

THE CENTURY CLASS
THE TRUCK FOR A NEW CENTURY

ABOVE Within four years, Freightliner reconsidered and redesigned more than 10,000 truck components when giving birth to the Century Class.

MANUFACTURER: Freightliner

TRUCK: Century Class

BBC: 112, 120 inches

DISTINCTIVE FEATURES: Supplemental restraint system incorporating a drop-away seat, driver's side air bag, and protective web restraint for drivers in the bunk

PREMIUM SLEEPER: 70-inch raised roof

Freightliner unveiled the pride of its line-up at the dawn of a new century. And indeed, the Century Class design marks a new direction for North America's largest truck builder. It took a 42-month development effort spanning two continents to develop the Century Class, with millions of dollars in research and development money spent while North America's trucking industry was in the grips of a recession. But this was an investment for the future. And it all began with senior vice-president of engineering and technology Michael von Mayenburg's rough, 22-page technical proposal for the truck that carried a code name of Premium 2.

The 120- and 112-inch conventionals can incorporate SleeperCabs ranging in size from a 48-inch mid-roof (a 58-inch version is standard) to an optional 70-inch raised-roof. Measuring 78 inches wide in front, the Century Class cab is also five inches wider than previous Freightliner designs, expanding to 83 inches at the B-pillar behind the doors, and to 91 inches in the sleeper.

Freightliner also wanted to maintain the classic look of a North American conventional with the Century Class, and shunned the idea of an overly sculpted design even when it looked to improve aerodynamics. Instead, the wind tunnel of Mercedes' research laboratory in Stuttgart, Germany, was used to enhance styling and the airflow under the hood designed in Freightliner's own vision, with the final truck sporting a 24-degree windshield angle and an integrated sun visor. The low-resistance grille and fender enclosures also manage to increase cooling capacity with the passing air, reducing the power draw associated with the engine fan and air conditioning.

ABOVE AND RIGHT The Century Class with a 70-inch raised roof sits on top of the lineup. Notice such distinctive features as the round headlights.

THE DRIVER'S LOUNGE
Added Comfort for the Century Class

Among sleeper options for the Century Class is the Driver's Lounge, which offers a sleeper that can easily be converted into an office on the road. The 39-inch bunk lifts and latches against the back wall to make room for a table that folds out from the underside of the bunk. Lifting the lower bunk reveals opposing bench-style seats. The table is large enough for two people to sit facing each other, has a center leg for added support, and has cut corners to make it easier for drivers to move around it. The Lounge can be ordered with 70-inch mid-roof and raised-roof cabs.

Airflow, however, doesn't play the only role in a truck's fuel efficiency. Ninety-five percent of the Century Class is made of aluminum, marking Freightliner's most extensive use of the material to shed weight. And where steel is used, such as in a front cross member, it's made of a hi-tech alloy. Chassis fairings are made with GTX nylon and the battery carrier is made of a fiber-reinforced polypropylene. An all-aluminum radiator does its part to shed the weight (22 pounds) and corrosion problems associated with brass cores. Seven-inch round headlamps not only round off the cab's look, but they're also easier to replace than other designs.

Initially, the Century Class was released as a "project in parallel" with a purpose-built Detroit Diesel Series 55 engine: a 12-liter, in-line, six-cylinder, turbocharged diesel power plant with air-to-air charge cooling. Detroit Diesel Corp. eventually dropped the engine design, however. Freightliner was preparing to replace the engine with a Mercedes design at the time of writing.

Meanwhile, designers also prepared for the worst. The Century Class was one of North America's first heavy-duty trucks to include an optional driver's-side air bag, but it was incorporated as only one element in a completely

BELOW Overhead storage helps store all the amenities of a home away from home.

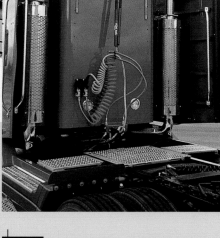

THE BACKPACK

Pushing Storage Past the Cab's Limits

Space is at a premium—even in top-notch conventional trucks. That's why Freightliner developed its Backpack. Located against the back wall of the sleeper, between dual upright exhausts, the storage option offers more space without ordering a larger cab. The Backpack adds 16.6 cubic feet of storage space in mid-roof models, and 27 cubic feet in raised-roof models.

The lower storage area is hidden behind sliding doors on the back wall of the sleeper, providing a hanging clothes compartment and additional shelves. On raised-roof models, two upper bunk storage bins are added.

The exterior of its roof even offers a protected pocket for satellite antennae.

ABOVE A prototype sleeper known as the Penthouse comes complete with lounge chairs.

redesigned restraint system. On impact, the driver's seatbelt is designed to tighten, with the seat itself dropping back and away from both the steering wheel and roof. A tent-style webbed restraint for sleeping passengers is designed to be less restrictive than traditional belts.

North America still hadn't developed a crash criterion of its own when the Century Class was unveiled, but the truck met with the European standards of ECE R-29. And to enhance safety further, the steering shaft was made to collapse, dash switches were softened and rounded, upper and lower bunks incorporated security latches, and fuel tanks were given more ground clearance.

When it came to details, refinements could be found in several areas. Handholds were located inside the cab with low-intensity illumination in the footwell; dome and reading lights were located over both seats; storage compartments were illuminated; and dual-intensity fluorescent lights were added to the sleeper. Interiors are available in several combinations of vinyl and cloth.

The Driver Message Center in the dashboard offers information on everything from trips, fuel use, and engine operation, to diagnostics and specific warnings for such conditions as vehicle operation with the parking brake applied, low oil pressure, low coolant level, low voltage, and high coolant temperature. Long-stroke brake chambers are standard equipment, while optional features range from front disc brakes to headlamp cleaning systems, and an Eaton-VORAD collision warning system.

With it all, the Century Class is ready to roll in the twenty-first century.

LEFT North America didn't have crash criterion of its own when the Century Class was designed, so Freightliner turned to the standards used to test its Mercedes brethren.

BELOW With chrome trim and other options, this Century Class package was unveiled for owner/operators.

THE ARGOSY
AN "UNCONVENTIONAL" COE

ABOVE The Argosy was unveiled in conjunction with a safety concept vehicle that married state-of-the-art components such as collision warning devices and lane departure systems to a 58-foot Wabash trailer with a specially designed rear axle that dropped only when it was needed.

MANUFACTURER: Freightliner

TRUCK: Argosy

BBC: 63, 90, 101, 110 inches

DISTINCTIVE FEATURES: Special retracting stairs make it easier than ever to access a cabover's cab

PREMIUM SLEEPER: 110-inch raised roof

Freightliner wanted to take an "unconventional" approach in the launch of its Argosy COE truck. That's obvious: look no further than the first steps into the cab, with the optional staircase that will swing out with the opening of the door. Ladders are a thing of the past.

The Argosy is built on a chassis and has components common to Century Class conventionals. It boasts a doghouse rising as little as three inches from the floor when lower-displacement engines are used, and seven inches when incorporated with power displacing more than 14 liters. That means no more climbing over a large hump in the middle of the cab when moving from the driver's seat to the sleeper.

The 110-inch BBC Argosy employs a 40-inch mid-axle setting for the front axle—balancing ride quality with a tight turning radius—and has a 183-inch wheelbase. Meanwhile, it is available in four BBC measurements and three roof configurations, including the 63-inch flat roof; 90-, 101-, and 110-inch mid-roof; and 110-inch raised roof.

An "unconventional" approach, however, also requires an "unconventional" shape. Aerodynamics are rarely highlighted in the launch of North American cabovers; they're the bricks of the Interstate highway system. But relying on a Mercedes wind

tunnel, the Argosy's aerodynamics managed to better those of its predecessor, the FLB, by 10 to 12 percent.

For that matter, the redesigned airflow helps in a number of ways. Air intakes located to the left and right of the grille move air by the engine and vent it across the bottom of the door, serving as a way to separate road spray from the windows and West Coast mirrors. Cooling air is drawn from an air intake which is located at the rear of the cab.

The 80-percent aluminum cab, meanwhile, also incorporates a bolt-on aluminum firewall common to the Century Class, along with other common components. And a service panel at the front tilts up 120 degrees for daily inspections, fluid fills, and bulkhead component repairs.

Inside, the dash has the distinct look of a Century Class design, with burlwood inserts, oversize gauges, and an integrated cup and vacuum flask holder. Auxiliary gauges and switches are located on the B-panel. And side spaces are used to include modular cabinets, a pull-out workstation, and other amenties. A sleeper booster unit on the heating, ventilation, and air-conditioning system is designed to help maintain

THE SMARTSHIFT

Fingertip Controls for a Sureshift

Traditional shift levers such as this one are mounted to the floor of an Argosy or Century Class. Freightliner's SmartShift has moved shifting to a wheel-mounted paddle. This is linked to Mentor's Sureshift automated transmission, and allows drivers to make upshifts by pulling back on the device, and downshifts by pushing forward. An LCD panel shows the gears that are available and, thanks to Sureshift technology, the clutch is only needed for starting and stopping.

an interior temperature in the face of ambient temperatures swinging from -20 to 105° Fahrenheit.

The cab itself meets European ECE R-29 structural load requirements, which hit a truck with a pendulum from the front, load the roof, and crush the back wall.

But perhaps the future of the Argosy shouldn't be considered without the experimental Wabash trailer that was launched with it. Freightliner president Jim Hebe had high expectations for this truck during its 1998 launch, particularly in his bid to convince the U.S. government to allow 58-foot trailers and 90,000-pound gross vehicle weights. There's little question that the American trucking industry has felt hamstrung by the lowest regulated weights in North America, with 53-foot maximum trailer lengths and the 80,000-pound tandem configurations that have become the industry's norm. But this high-cube trailer boasted an interior load height of 10 feet 1½ inches, yet retained an overall height of 13 feet 6½ inches when the Argosy was fitted with low-profile wheels.

Legislators would be "scared to death" of expanding the use of double- and triple-trailer combinations, he said. But perhaps they'd allow longer trailers with trucks such as the extensively apportioned Argosy known as the Safety Concept Vehicle. Its electronic brake-by-wire system was married with wide-track axles and low-profile tires, and there was the prototype of a lane departure system that buzzes at drivers when the truck strays from its lane. An Eaton VORAD EVT 300 collision warning system was linked to an adaptive cruise control to ensure a safe following distance was always maintained. To help distribute weight and turn the longer trailer design, a rear axle located behind a standard tandem set of wheels was designed to steer and lift as sensors indicated a need. And with a six-foot kingpin setting, the distance from the kingpin to the center line of the trailer still met the U.S. state of California's maximum dimension of 41 feet. At the time of writing, there was still a question over whether the longer lengths would become a reality. But its builders were ever hopeful. Said Hebe, "I think there's a 50/50 chance of it happening."

LEFT With a lower engine tunnel—known to truckers as the doghouse—it's easier to move about the cab.

RIGHT Access to the cab is eased with optional self-retracting steps (1), the aerodynamically-friendly design (2), the service panel tilts open 120 degrees for daily inspection and to fill fluids (3), engine servicing is possible with both a tilt of the cab and the lifting of a service panel (4).

1

2

3

4

THE FLD
CONVENTIONAL THINKING

ABOVE True to its roots, Freightliner incorporates an extensive use of lightweight components in the FLD.

MANUFACTURER: Freightliner

TRUCK: FLD

BBC: 112, 120 inches

DISTINCTIVE FEATURES: Signature fiberglass composite hood

PREMIUM SLEEPER: 70-inch raised roof

Freightliner's FLD 112 and 120 truck lines are among the most popular vehicles on North American highways. Incorporating a set-forward front axle, the design features its signature fiberglass composite hood that slopes down seven degrees for improved visibility. Dual five-inch, cab-mounted exhausts with curved vertical tailpipes, chrome upper stacks, and stainless-steel muffler shields round out the look.

Down below, a rolled-under bumper is built in three pieces that can be replaced separately, and includes recessed areas with room for three licence plates and fog lamps, not forgetting a center tow pin/step. And moving up the hood, the front turn signal is integrated into the side of the headlamp assembly's housing, while the trademark grille is made of anodized aluminum.

Enhancing the view from the cab are stainless-steel 7 x 16 West Coast mirrors attached to brackets for 102-inch trailers, including lower struts designed to keep the mirrors from vibrating. Structurally, the cab's riveted aluminum panels are reinforced with steel in high-stress areas.

Fuel efficiency isn't forgotten in the conventional with the look of a traditional conventional, however. Aerodynamics are further improved with flush-mounted

handles in the insulated aluminum bulkhead doors. And cab side extenders can close the gap between cabs and trailers, cutting out a traditional source of turbulence. Side fairings can direct airflow down the lower side of the cab, and also have the ability to reduce splash and spray. Rear-mounted exhausts can also be specified.

Access to the back of the cab, meanwhile, is eased with steps that run along the length of the side fairing. Inside, the ride is enhanced with Soft Rate taperleaf front springs and a shock-absorbing cab suspension, with an optional AirLiner rear air suspension.

Electrical needs are covered in a number of areas. The jump start post, for example, is located on the left front cab mount for easy access, while three maintenance-free batteries can be expanded with an optional fourth. The bus bar stored behind an access panel under the center of the woodgrain-covered dash also offers room for as many as 24 circuit breakers.

At the top of the line of 13 different sleeper configurations is the 70-inch raised-roof SleeperCab, where the ceiling soars to eight feet and a 15½ x 33½-inch skylight lets the sun shine in. Interiors vary from Premier Vinyl to a Premier Cloth, Benchmark Cloth, and Custom Vinyl. Double standard bunks are coupled with extensive storage, cool fluorescent lighting, and 12-volt connectors for a TV, cooler, or other appliances. And storage space includes a wide array of options, including a 14 x 28-inch hanging storage cabinet for the 48-inch SleeperCab; wraparound shelving for a 58- and 70-inch mid-roof; and an optional rear-wall closet for raised-roof models. They all help offer a home away from home.

ABOVE Built for the long haul, an FLD 120's sleeper can offer many home comforts.

BELOW Unlike the Century Class that followed it, the FLD incorporates squared headlights.

THE CLASSIC XL
A LOOK OF LUXURY

MANUFACTURER: Freightliner

TRUCK: Classic XL

BBC: 132-inches

DISTINCTIVE FEATURES: Long-nose conventional with set-forward front axles

PREMIUM SLEEPER: 70-inch Sleeper Cab

BELOW Fully specified with a package of options, the Classic XL offers the aggressive look of a traditional long-nosed conventional.

For truck owners seeking the look of a long-nose conventional, Freightliner offers the Classic XL. With a 132-inch BBC, the aggressive-looking front end is complemented with trim options ranging from a collection of chrome, polish, and custom paint jobs. And there's plenty of room under the hood for engines pulling with the power of as many as 600 horses.

This is a truck for those who want to live in the world of pride and shine, with a wide array of seating options in five different interior levels and 21 different colors. At the top of the line is a new Classic Chaparral upholstery package and a 70-inch raised-roof SleeperCab, although the wide array of sleeper options ranges right back to the 40-inch sleeper box.

ABOVE The Classic XL design ensures that it can be equipped with the highest horsepower engines on the market and the transmissions to go with them (above left and right). But the interior with its Classic Chaparral upholstery package and wood-grained dash (below left and right) offers premium comfort as well.

NEXT PAGE With its 132-inch BBC and a set-forward steering axle, the Classic XL is a prime example of the classic long-nosed conventional.

IVECO
ITALY

Spread from Turin, Italy, to Madras, India, and Nanjing, China, IVECO is truly an international endeavor. But it all began in Italy when FIAT built its first commercial vehicle in 1902. The delivery van was powered with an 8-hp, 1.9-liter vertical-twin engine, a three-speed gearbox, and side chain drive. And a heavier truck came in 1903 with the four-ton model that rolled forward on iron tires. Its driver sat above the 6.3-liter T-head engine mounted ahead of the front axle, moving at a maximum speed of 7.5 mph.

By 1927, FIAT controlled 80 percent of Italy's domestic commercial truck market, only two years after absorbing SPA. In 1931 it took over OM (Società Anonima Officine Meccaniche, formed in Turin, Italy), followed by Bianchi in 1955, and Lancia in 1968. The Industrial Vehicle Corporation (IVECO) was formed in 1975, also incorporating Magirus Deutz Motoren AG. Today, IVECO builds one in every five commercial vehicles on the roads of Western Europe and has made more than 2 million vehicles, selling in excess of 150,000 trucks per year. The division of the Fiat Group is one of the world's largest manufacturers of diesel engines.

BELOW EuroStar is the star of the Iveco range, made for heavy, long-distance hauls.

THE EUROTECH
DESIGNED TO GO THE DISTANCE

When IVECO wanted to build a cab for high-mileage operators, it looked to the design talents of Giuiaro. The result: 1993 Truck of the Year honors for the EuroTech. More than 900 versions of the truck's modular design help comply with the restrictions on lengths that can vary widely from one country to the next, and provide a wide array of designs for specialty applications. Highway, tipper/dog, general, and B-double or road trains can all be configured, with gross combination weights ranging between 32 and 90 tons. And all of the versions—whether the medium-heavy (MT) or heavy (MP) models—fit the company's modular cabs.

The cabs themselves are available in a short version with a normal or high roof (top sleeper), or 83 inches long with a normal or medium roof. And when specified, the sleeper can incorporate twin bunks, the top of which will fold out of the way when not in use. The range is completed with a choice of wheelbase lengths, with body lengths of up to 30 feet; optimized for pallets and mobile crates.

Entry into the cab is eased with the first step located just 14³/₄ inches from the ground. And once inside, a panoramic view is offered not only through a large laminated windshield but also through low-cut door windows and a deep curb observation window.

A contoured bumper and under-bumper air dam not only helps improve aerodynamics but reduces noise and protects the recessed headlamps from minor

ABOVE There are more than 900 versions of the truck's modular design to help comply with varying national length restrictions.

MANUFACTURER: IVECO

TRUCK: EuroTech

DISTINCTIVE FEATURES: A modular design with 900 versions to meet varying length laws

PREMIUM SLEEPER: 83-inch cab

knocks. After all, the cab has been built to last. About 40 percent of it has been made from rust-resistant SMC, including the front panel, grille, corner panels, roof section, steps, and wheel wells. The remainder is treated to resist corrosion.

The spare wheel is mounted on the chassis side of the truck, along with a weight-reducing fuel tank, while air tanks are accessed on the side of the chassis which holds an additional tank for air drying and automatic water blow down, plus brake and anti-freeze equipment. Air tanks for the suspension are located adjacent to their associated axles.

In terms of power, engines include six-cylinder in-line units that are turbocharged with an intercooler in 7.7-, 9.5-, and 13.8-liter sizes, offering between 266 and 420 hp. But sometimes there's a greater need to control whatever power is available. A differential lock with electropneumatic control is available as a standard component on the MP and is optional on the MT, to meet the needs of long-haul drivers who can find themselves in a variety of environments. Acceleration Spin Control (ASR), meanwhile, helps the truck grip slick roads during acceleration by countering slipping wheels. By using the same sensors that control the rig's anti-lock brakes, the ASR applies brake pressure if one wheel begins to slip. And in very severe cases, when both wheels are spinning, overall power is cut completely with the automated limiting of the fuel supply.

In the event of maintenance problems, a fascia-mounted Check Control diagnostic system offers drivers an early warning to pre-empt catastrophic problems. And once service is needed, maintenance is eased with a cab that hydraulically tilts to 67 degrees, and power is ensured through a high-performance 55-amp alternator and starter motors with outputs ranging from 4.0 to 6.6 kilowatts.

For the demanding environs of Australia, the same Iveco engines and European-style cabs are married to more robust North American drivetrains. Every truck in the range is fitted with a strong, light chassis that incorporates parallel longitudinal beams, and a simple "bottleneck" on MT models and double "bottleneck" on MP models, with the front of the chassis designed to accommodate larger engines. IVECO axles offer a 52-degree steering angle. Hubs with disc brakes are set for ABS. It is, after all, designed to go the distance.

THE EUROSTAR
A STAR ATTRACTION

Without a doubt, the EuroStar is the star of the Iveco range, made for the demands of heavy, long-distance hauls. The truck is built around a frame covered with steel panels that are galvanized where they're exposed to the elements, or SMC, a synthetic material that won't corrode. Five wheelbases offer an array of ways to exploit the length of the truck's body, including a design that meets the needs of 44-foot 9-inch semi-trailers allowed in the new European Union code.

It's purposely been built for robust applications—for B-double, highway, road train, or general loads ranging from gross combination weights of 72 to 90 tons. And the short wheelbase offers room for maximum-length, 34-pallet trailers.

Under it all is the power of engines ranging between 420 and the 514-hp turbocharged and intercooled V8.

The cab measures 8 feet wide, 6 feet 9½ inches long, and has more than 7½ feet of standing height in the high-roof version, not to mention four-point air

ABOVE The robust nature of a EuroStar makes it capable of attacking long hauls through Eastern Europe and the roads of the former Soviet Union that have become a reality since the collapse of the Iron Curtain. Now there's no mountain that's too high.

MANUFACTURER: IVECO

TRUCK: EuroStar

DISTINCTIVE FEATURES: Robust design built for B-double, highway, road train or general loads

PREMIUM SLEEPER: 81½-inch cab

The EuroStar's short wheelbae offers a configuration that is capable of handling maximum-length, 34-pallet trailers.

Gears are changed without the clutch when using the SAMT.

suspension with leveling valves. Door handles are positioned low, with three deep, non-slip illuminated steps, the first of which is only 13 inches from the ground. The door itself will open 90 degrees, with intermediate stop-and-grab handles positioned on both sides of the doorway. The full-width cab will still tilt a full 72 degrees for ease of servicing.

A semi-automated mechanical transmission (SAMT) is standard on 520-hp models and optional elsewhere, helping the truck stay running in the optimal double-green zone of the tachometer. With it, the clutch is only moved to start moving or to stop, with three electropneumatic cylinders doing all the shifting-related work. Shifts are made with a fingertip-operated selector that replaces the conventional gear lever, with a display confirming the selection of gears.

For those who prefer synchromesh gearboxes, the EuroStar 380 and 420 hp models offer the ZF 16-speed EcoSplit. And on 380 and 420-hp models, those who want constant mesh can choose an Eaton 12-speed twin splitter.

The steering wheel is height- and rake-adjustable. And with an air suspension, the seat's height, lumbar support, and the longitudinal position of the cushion can all be adjusted. A small container mounted between the seats acts both as an insulated container and steps for easier access into the bunk's sleeping compartment.

The sleeper has no side windows—keeping the light of day out—while electric rollup sunshades are fitted on the side windows and windshield to ensure that any bedtime is uninterrupted.

THE EUROTRONIC TRANSMISSION
The Joy of Shifting with a Joystick

For those tired of gear jamming and the ever-pressing need to press a clutch, IVECO's EuroTronic automated clutch takes over. The EuroTronic's electropneumatic clutch has no pedal, and gears are changed with a joystick-style lever. A dash-mounted display tells the driver what shifts are available, and changes are made simply by pushing forward for an upshift and pulling back for a downshift. Skip shifting is accomplished by touching the lever twice consecutively. If you change down two gears, the control unit that monitors the operation of the gearbox will only engage the gear when the engine is at the correct speed.

A function button adds to the control. Depress it and push the joystick forward two positions and the EuroTronic selects a gear in the peak torque. Hold it and pull it one step back, and there's maximum power. Pull the T-bar back two positions and the system chooses the maximum available engine revolutions. Although full control remains in the driver's hands, it won't allow transmission-damaging over-revving.

The 12-speed EuroTronic 1800 equips the EuroTech and EuroStar ranges in combinations with the 380 bhp engine, and the 16-speed EuroTronic 2000 is available on the EuroStar engine with the 470 bhp engine. The final product weighs 88 to 123 pounds less than a conventional gearbox. And external cables have been reduced to a single power line.

When the EuroTronic is coupled with a hydraulic retarder, there's the added benefit of less wear on brake pads. The initial pick-up with a heavy or poor load betters that of a conventional gearbox because there are no synchronizers involved in the process.

Still, there has to be an allowance for any system to break down. An auxiliary limp-home function is a mechanical system that bypasses the electronic control unit in the event of a fault.

Standard equipment also includes athermic, blue-tinted glass; central door locking; and electrically adjustable exterior mirrors with a demister. For the driver, a ceiling-high strip includes electric mirror controls and the radio and CB housing complete with speakers. An electronic instrument panel has been located to place the tachometer and speedometer at the center of the driver's vision, with gauges to the right measuring water temperature, fuel level, oil, and brake circuit pressure. Telltale alarms are positioned at the top of the instrument panel.

ABOVE High-roof versions of the cab offer a generous 84½ inches of standing height.

The levels of engine oil, coolant, screen-washing liquid, and the brake circuit air-hydraulic system can be checked by raising the front grille 120 degrees (it's counterweighted by double dampers). And the cab tilts 72 degrees with a hydraulic jack for serious repairs, while an electric pump is available with a double safety system. To make it easier to detach the cab from the rest of the vehicle, the electrical system is equipped with an interconnecting element, which is really a multipole macro socket. Half of it is permanently connected to the front cab bulkhead, while the other half acts as the terminal of the system wiring.

The best maintenance, however, is the work that is never required. Oil changes have been extended to once every 31,000 miles, and the only lubrication points are in the wheel bearings and steering joints. Leaf spring attachments don't need maintenance at all.

THE TRANSTAR 4700
EXCLUSIVE TO AUSTRALIA

Through its International Trucks subsidiary, IVECO's truck range includes a conventionally styled option popular with the high-horsepower needs of Australia. The 6 x 4 Transtar 4700s are the pride of the range, well equipped for the requirements of linehaul, B-double, heavy-haul, road train double and triple combinations. With a gross vehicle mass of 24.4 to 30.3 tons, its allowable gross combination weight stretches from 50 to 130 tons.

Aerodynamics for long-haul fuel efficiency are improved right from the bonneted snout down to the elimination of protruding air cleaners and air horns that offer the added bonus of easier cleaning.

Among the cab choices are a day cab with external lockers or the optional premium sleeper cab. The steel cab itself measures 90 inches wide, offering more room for visibility and stowage, with a fiberglass tilting hood and fenders. Exterior panels are double-sided zinc-coated steel in the cab with a 113½-inch BBC as standard, with a 143½-inch BBC with the sleeper.

The cab itself rides on an air suspension mounted at the rear of the cab, while the driver's seat features self-leveling air suspensions with fore and aft isolators, as well as adjustments for inclination, lumbar support, and longitudinal movement. Cruise control is a standard option with this cab.

Lockable storage space can be found under each seat, with two more mounted under the floor, while both external compartments lock from inside the cab. A manifest holder situated on the rear of the engine tunnel is also available.

Standard appointments include a 10-liter Engel refrigerator with a padded lid, a mobile phone, CB radio, engine idle timer, and a Blend Air air conditioner with a three-speed fan and demister. An array of gauges includes the speedometer, odometer, tachometer, volt meter, fuel level, oil pressure, water temperature, air pressure (two), engine, transmission, and rear-axle oil temperature, hazard lights, and more.

Integral sleepers have shorter BBC sizes than add-on dog boxes, meaning the fifth wheel is set far enough forward to allow for the maximum allowable load on the front axle. And with the integrated design, drivers don't have to crawl through a hole in the wall to get into the sleeper. On one side is an adjustable reading lamp, and on the other an electric fan with a side clothes closet with elasticized pockets on the door and quarter panel.

A sleeper console incorporates an ashtray, cigarette lighter, cigarette pack holder, electric fan switch, radio volume control, a socket for headphones, a low voltage monitor, a digital alarm clock, dome light switch, and a magazine rack. Three

RIGHT Keeping cool in the Australian outback.

MANUFACTURER: International

TRUCK: Transtar 4700

BBC: 113½, 143½ inches

DISTINCTIVE FEATURES: A hood that's still sloped for maximum visibility and aerodynamics

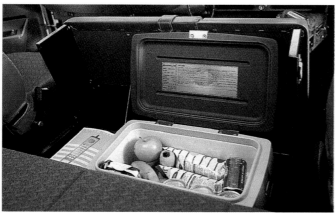

ABOVE As a model designed exclusively for Australia, the Transtar 4700 is standard with right-hand drive.

RIGHT Protruding air horns and air cleaners are removed to improve aerodynamics, and offer the added benefit of easier cleaning.

KENWORTH TRUCK CO.
SEATTLE, WASHINGTON, U.S.A.

Kenworth's roots can be traced to brothers Louis and Edgar Gerlinger, who founded the Gerlinger Motor Car Company in Portland, Oregon, in 1912. But since there were as yet few cars on the road during their early days in business, they filled time in the garage by building a truck called the Gersix. The design was meant to handle the steep grades common to the terrain of the Pacific Northwest, and it sported a six-cylinder Continental engine when most of its competitors had a four-cylinder engine.

When the first 2½-ton version was sold in 1915, a new trucking business was born. Although the business struggled, it was bought in 1917 by Seattle-based investors including Edgar K. Worthington. And following the later addition of partner Harry Kent, Worthington placed the first KW nameplate on the nose of a truck in 1923. Among its many achievements, the company boasted the first North American factory installation of a diesel engine, which took place in 1933. And today, the Kenworth nameplate can be found from the oil fields of the Middle East to the timberlands of the Philippines, and into the coal mining areas of Australia.

In its seventy-fifth year in 1998, the company was producing trucks in Seattle and Renton, Washington State; Chillicothe, Ohio; Mexicali, Mexico; Bayswater, Victoria, Australia; and Xuzhou, Jiangsu, China. It was also preparing to re-open a plant in Ste-Thérèse, Quebec, Canada, in 1999.

ABOVE AND BELOW Kenworth's unconventional snout on the T600 wasn't shown in the early concept vehicles. Until length laws changed, the company was planning a new cabover design. The hoods on North American models (below) now make each aerodynamic design readily identifiable.

THE T600
AN UNCONVENTIONAL CONVENTIONAL

Engineer Larry Orr wasn't met with the warmest reception when he drove the first T600A to Kenworth headquarters. Some executives just shook their heads when they saw the drastically sculpted design. But Orr was right and he knew he had a winner.

Without a doubt, Kenworth shocked the world of trucking in 1985 when it unveiled a radical design that could be described as nothing less than an unconventional conventional. But its design enhancements didn't end there. Several improvements were unveiled four years later with the T600, including the Aerodyne II aerodynamic sleeper and further enhancements such as a sculpted sun visor with flush-mounted marker and clearance lights. Aerodynamic mirrors with a "breakaway" low-profile mounting bracket were added along with a one-piece curved windshield. Such changes improved the fuel economy of the original T600A by six-and-a-half percent. And that's quite an achievement considering the original 22 percent improvement over previous Kenworth conventionals.

In 1992, the B-model cab was unveiled with a curved windshield. And in 1993 came the T600 AeroCab, with a new contoured cab roof, integrated side panels, and a redesigned chassis fairing that reduced drag by yet another three percent.

ABOVE Until changes in the regulations governing weights and dimensions, Kenworth's new truck was going to be an aerodynamic cabover.

MANUFACTURER: Kenworth

TRUCK: T600

DISTINCTIVE FEATURES: An award-winning aerodynamic design that gave a new look to conventional wisdom

PREMIUM SLEEPER: 72-inch AeroCab

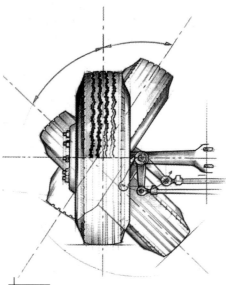

ABOVE In addition to relying on the sloped hood, aerodynamics are further improved by sculpted fenders (1), air dam under the bumper (2), and even the mirror designs (3, 4).

ABOVE The truck's 46-inch setback front axle and 165-inch wheelbase makes a 56-foot turning circle possible.

The T600's sloped hood not only offers better aerodynamics, but also improves the visibility offered by other conventional designs. And the contoured shape ends in an upturned sweep to direct the wind up and over the curved windshield. The bumper, too, is formed with aerodynamics in mind, to direct the air under and around the cab. Another significant improvement over the T600A is something you can't sense. The Quiet Cab insulation package unveiled in 1992 cut interior noise by half.

In terms of dimensions, the 46-inch setback front axle maximizes the potential payload, transferring more weight to the front end and increasing the ability to turn the truck in tighter spaces. With a 165-inch wheelbase, the curb-to-curb turning circle is trimmed to 56 feet. And with 12,000 pounds on the front axle, the truck can pull the American standard GVW of 80,000 pounds without the deep fifth-wheel settings that can compromise ride quality. (For that matter, the 64-inch taperleaf front springs and outboard-mounted shocks, air springs, and a transverse lateral control rod have also cushioned the impact of long rides.)

For long hauls, the angle of the toe-board is flatter than that of many trucks, helping reduce leg strain, while an optional Easy Reach dash puts toggle switches close at hand. An optional Electronic Dash brings in the digital age with a simulated analog look that helps diagnose engine faults and document mileage. With the SmartWheel, 11 frequently used controls over such things as engine retarders, cruise control, headlamps, and marker lights are all placed at the driver's fingertips.

Sleeper options include a 60-inch Aerodyne, or 60- and 42-inch FlatTop units. Low-profile and raised-roof cabs are available for a variety of applications, and the AeroCab, as already stated, reduces aerodynamic drag by another three percent over

LEFT While the original T600A bettered the fuel economy of other designs by 22 percent, improvements in the T600 bettered that by another 6½ percent. Aerodynamics, of course, played a crucial role.

ABOVE The sloped hood and pepper window in the passenger door enhance the driver's view of the road ahead.

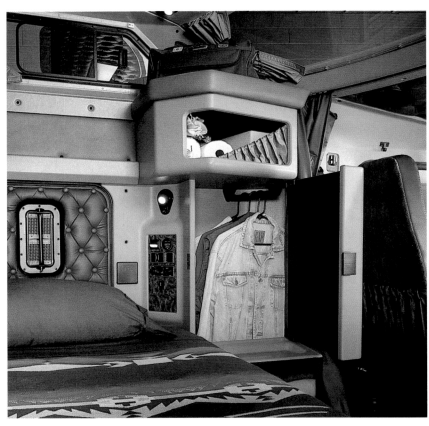

LEFT The AeroCab offers the space of a 72-inch modular sleeper in a more compact and lighter package.

ABOVE Kenworth has made a name for itself that has pushed from its home in the Pacific Northwest, across the Rocky Mountains and onto other continents. Its models include this 84-inch high contoured roofline of the 72-inch AeroCab Aerodyne VIT incorporates Vista windows for natural light.

the T600. The AeroCab offers the space of a 72-inch modular sleeper in a more compact and lighter package. Its seven-foot-high contoured roofline with a lowered sleeper floor adds to the space. And the traditional bulkhead between sleepers and cabs is shed to include more space for the seat to travel, offering more elbow, leg, and belly room.

For those needing a lower profile, a 72-inch AeroCab FlatTop VIT offers all the comforts of home. And there's even stand-up room for a six-foot driver. The 72-inch AeroCab Aerodyne VIT offers five more inches of headroom in the cab, while the sleeper's 84-inch-high contoured roofline incorporates Vista windows for natural light. A 42-inch mattress, floor lighting, and additional center storage console in the cab add to the sleeper's amenities that include a TV installation package, cabinet drawers, under-bunk drawers, a front-loading refrigerator, rear sleeper window, and a folding upper bunk. More VIT storage features include a full-length clothes closet, cabinets with doors and drawers, and a tuck-away desk. The attention to detail certainly wasn't limited to the exterior.

THE W900L
A CONVENTIONAL DESIGN TO BE SHOWCASED

The truck maker that wins awards for aerodynamic designs isn't about to abandon the straight-hood conventional that is a showcase of its line-up. Kenworth's W900L measures 130 inches from the bumper to the back of the cab and is one of the longest long-nosed conventionals on the road.

First introduced in 1963, the W900 has seen several updates since then. In 1976, the VIT Aerodyne sleeper added to the comfort, and in 1982 it received a redesigned cab. Three years later, a new generation of sleepers featured a lowered floor and bulkhead doors for easier access. The W900L offered an extended hood 10 inches longer than that of the W900B in the 1990s. But even with its stretched profile, the location of the stearing gear ahead of the front axle enhances the turning radius of the truck. Then in late 1993 there was the addition of the W900 Studio Sleeper, while the AeroCab came in 1994.

In-cab storage includes a spot for a vacuum flask, upholstered pockets behind the seats, a slide-in logbook and pen holder, an under-the-dash multifunction center console with a built-in coffee cup recess, and more.

MANUFACTURER:	Kenworth
TRUCK:	W900L
BBC:	130 inches
DISTINCTIVE FEATURES:	An aggressive-looking hood 10 inches longer than the W900B's hood
PREMIUM SLEEPER:	86-inch Studio AeroCab

BELOW For those who prefer to travel the show 'n shine circuit, well-chromed W900Ls have proven to be winners. Kenworth tightened the steering radius of the W900L by placing the steering gear ahead of the front axle.

When it comes to a home away from home, there's a 72-inch modular sleeper in a compact package with five more inches of headroom in the cab. Alternatively there's the 74-inch Studio Sleeper, incorporating a fold-out sofa bed. Inside, the 72-inch AeroCab Aerodyne VIT, with its seven-foot contoured roofline, contains more than 70 cubic feet of storage space. There's wall-to-wall carpeting and a hanging clothes closet, a cabinet with two shelves, a fold-down desk, an overbunk storage console in the cab, and a 42-inch mattress. The under-bunk drawers, liftable lower bunk, rear and side sleeper windows, and a front-loading refrigerator/freezer all add to the comfort.

But as with any showcase truck, it's the options that can help enhance this vehicle's look. A wide array of stainless steel additions include: a Kenworth nameplate behind the fender; door kick panels; a frame for the shift boot; cowl-mounted air cleaners from Donaldson, Farr, or Vortox; and quarter fenders. Then there are polished aluminum fuel tanks holding up to 150 gallons of fuel, traditional Kenworth gullwing or rectangular Texas-style chromed steel bumpers, and a stainless steel eyebrow that can be mounted over the headlamps. It may be built to work, but it shows with style.

THE T800
A TRUCK BUILT FOR THE RUGGED HAUL

Kenworth's T800 was built for the most rugged applications a highway can offer, with 120- or 112-inch BBC dimensions and a setback axle. The truck maker's most versatile product evolved from the sloped hood and setback axle design of the T600, but still meets the rugged needs of the construction industry and other vocational applications. And it's catching on. This is Kenworth Mexicana's best-selling truck. In 1992, the T800 was first offered with the Aerodyne II sleeper and, in 1993, the T800 Heavy Hauler featured a larger radiator and grille for 550-hp engines.

This is Kenworth's heavyweight, for GCWs up to 350,000 pounds and the high-horsepower engines that need the cooling capacity of a 1,520-square-inch radiator.

ABOVE The versatile T800 design is one of Kenworth's most popular trucks in Mexico.

MANUFACTURER: Kenworth

TRUCK: T800

BBC: 120, 112 inches

DISTINCTIVE FEATURES: A rugged design with a setback front axle

PREMIUM SLEEPER: Studio Aerocab

LEFT While sculpted for aerodynamics, the T800 has still been built to withstand heavyweight loads.

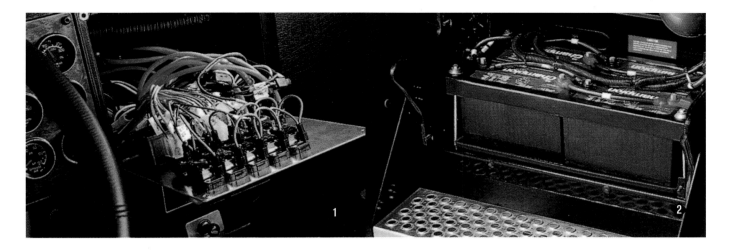

Front axles can be rated up to 22,000 pounds, while other options include factory-installed pusher axles and PTOs, dual power steering, a center-front tow hitch, sheet metal hood for severe service, and frame options offered in steel or aluminum, with or without inserts.

Even with its dominant hood, the T800 still offers a 25 percent tighter turning circle than that of standard Kenworth conventionals. The setback front axle and improved steering geometry deliver a 40-degree wheel cut. And the ride is handled by 64-inch taperleaf front springs, coupled with Kenworth's Cab Mate air suspension from Link Manufacturing.

But in rugged applications, rugged construction takes center stage. Rattles are reduced with huckbolts that offer six times the clamping force provided by normal rivets. Bulkhead-style doors hang on piano hinges, and their seals are mounted right to the door, where they can't be destroyed by dirt and workboots. The continuous straight frame is constructed of heat-treated steel, and extruded aluminum crossmembers and aluminum gussets add additional foundation without a lot of extra weight. (Optional hex-shaped huckbolt collars can be removed with a wrench, eliminating the labor and cost of cutting them off.)

For maintenance, the hood tilts 90 degrees for easy access to fluid fills, filters, and engine components. At the firewall—and within easy reach—are the heater/air-conditioner motor, electrical master connectors, windshield wiper motor, and washer reservoir.

The power distribution box is mounted to the left of the clutch pedal, putting circuit protection elements in one central, lit location. A modular dash panel tilts out to expose cab wiring and its coded wires, while front-loading gauges have push-on connections.

The 12-volt maintenance-free batteries are mounted in a corrosion-resistant, shock-absorbing rubber tray that's found on the left-hand side of the truck—in close proximity to the starter motor to minimize dropping voltage.

But decked out for shows, the T800 can also include factory-installed, signature-setting Kenworth exclusives such as polished battery boxes, tool boxes, and fuel tanks; stainless cowl-mounted air cleaners; dual polished vertical exhaust stacks; and lighted trim panels. It's built for work, but owners can still take pride in the look.

ABOVE (1) The modular dash panel tilts out for easy servicing, and (2) batteries are mounted close to the starter to minimize voltage drop.

BELOW Just because it's built for rugged work doesn't mean you can't travel in style.

ABOVE (1) The T800's durability also makes it popular as a (2) dump truck, (3) mixer, (4) or heavy-hauling day cab.

THE STUDIO AEROCAB
NORTH AMERICA'S SPACE LEADER

Kenworth's 86-inch Studio AeroCab leads the space race with a sleeper that could best be described as a studio apartment. It is the largest truck sleeper provided by an original equipment manufacturer.

The sofa pulls out into a 42-inch bunk and is surrounded by a top-of-the-line VIT interior package with wall-to-wall carpeting and a handstitched diamond interior available in various colors. Two full-length enclosed closets are standard, while a driver's side drawer offers extra clothes storage. (Closet shelves are also available.)

An alderwood table measuring 16 x 22 inches doubles as a work desk, while a built-in TV installation package allows room for an entertainment system.

There are fold-down cupholders near the side windows and a large-capacity refrigerator/freezer. And two sleeper windows are mounted on the side doors, while vista windows and large upper side windows let in the light until a vinyl curtain covers them when it's time to sleep.

ABOVE As North America's largest sleeper, the 86-inch studio AeroCab can even offer a couch.

LEFT Attached to a W900L—one of the longest of long-nosed conventionals—the Studio turns heads.

THE T2000
A SHAPE FOR A NEW MILLENNIUM

ABOVE Aerodynamics of the T2000 are improved with a rounded hood profile (1), sculpted fenders (2), smoothed fairings (3), sloped windshield (4), and even a sculpted bumper (5).

Aerodynamics were the focus of Kenworth's T600A unveiled in 1985, and the T2000 built on the ideas in 1996. The truck's dramatically rounded hood has a steeper slope and is six inches lower in front than the T600, while the windshield—with its 32-degree slope—is 64 percent larger than that of any other Kenworth model. The result means that in 11 years of design work, Kenworth managed to improve the fuel efficiency of its truck line by 30 percent.

Where engine cooling is a problem when using high-horsepower engines in the T600, that difficulty is solved in the T2000. A cross-flow radiator replaces traditional vertical designs. And with a radiator measuring 1,350 square inches, a 550-hp engine can be accommodated under the hood of a 120-inch BBC model, while a 112-inch BBC version can handle 11- and 12-liter engines.

Step through the door that opens 68 degrees for access to a cab measuring 84 inches from door to door, with 30 inches between the seats. Then there's 74 inches

of headroom between the seats, and 80 inches of headroom at the highest point in the Aerodyne sleeper. The view outside is further improved with a teardrop-shape window and peeper windows in the Daylight 2 door, while West Coast mirrors on the passenger side of the truck are 1½ inches higher than those on the driver's side.

Each door incorporates a window cassette with most of the door mechanisms including the glass, run channels, and window regulators. Remove 10 screws and the cassette can be lifted out for servicing.

Meanwhile, the truck with a space-age look has also incorporated space-age materials. A sheet-molded compound is used for the hood and roof cap, while a new one-piece ThermaCore floor and epoxy-based chassis side fairings shed weight. The exterior lines of the truck are further improved by eliminating external fasteners and overlapping seams, replacing them with an advanced urethane adhesive and aircraft-style, self-piercing fasteners.

MANUFACTURER: Kenworth

TRUCK: T2000

BBC: 112, 120 inches

DISTINCTIVE FEATURES: Rounded, aerodynamic shape and better visibility

PREMIUM SLEEPER: Aerodyne

ABOVE Daylight shines through both Vista and side windows, flooding the sleeper.

Inside, a wraparound dash incorporates the radio and CB, taking them out of the header. The main instrument panel includes electronic gauges with built-in warning lights, and a standard LCD multifunction display in the center offers a main odometer, four trip odometers, information on the percent of throttle, fault codes displayed in real English, and an alarm clock.

Lighting includes three lamps in the header for ambient light, and spotlights on both the driver and passenger sides of the cab. A utility tray is meant to hold drinks in place while an optional center console is left with room for satellite keyboards, a place for roadmaps and paperwork, and a logbook storage compartment. At 15 degrees to the driver are rocker switch controls for headlamps, cruise control, engine brakes, and more, with room for up to nine additional gauges.

In terms of the ride, the eight-bag Airglide 200 air suspension incorporates a parallelogram, multilink design that lets axles stay at constant angles as they move up and down, cutting down on torque-induced vibration in the driveline. In terms of

strength, the ten ⅝-inch frame rails and 16-mm bolts improve upon 12-mm bolts used in the T600's construction.

The heating, ventilation, and air-conditioning system includes several improvements on its own. A centrally located defrosting outlet on the firewall shoots air across the windshield instead of up and over, keeping it out of the driver's face. And with the system mounted to the firewall instead of behind the dash, servicing is easier. The evaporator core, heater core, blower motor, and filter are all easily accessed, and the entire unit can be removed with six bolts, with hoses that will stretch far enough to rest the system on a workbench. For those who take their dog along for the ride, the filter incorporated into the HVAC system will even keep pet hair out of heater cores.

The central electrical panel is located behind the glove compartment and incorporates 16 additional circuits, while the battery box is hidden under fairings below the driver's side door, close to the starter motor for a minimal drop in voltage. After all, it's built with power in mind.

KENWORTH AUSTRALIA
THE T604
HIGH EFFICIENCY FOR HIGH HORSES

ABOVE Although its shape is similar to the T2000, the T604 offers additional capacity for engine cooling required in Australia.

MANUFACTURER: Kenworth

TRUCK: T604

DISTINCTIVE FEATURES: Cooling capacity that can handle 122°F at 15 mph

PREMIUM SLEEPER: T604 Aero 50

Combining high horsepower with an aerodynamic design isn't an easy task. Truck designs with sculpted fronts invariably lead to smaller grilles—and that can mean limited cooling abilities. However, Kenworth Australia says it has designed the best of both worlds in the T604.

Designed and manufactured at a plant in Melbourne, Australia, the truck replaces the T601 and boasts a cooling package capable of handling the most powerful on-highway engines on the market.

Moving the engine to improve the clearance between the fan and the rear of the radiator core enhanced the design's cooling abilities. The size of the engine bay was increased to improve the effectiveness of the fan, while a streamlined radiator shroud was also introduced. And the cab height was raised to improve the air flow under the

hood, while molded fiberglass splash shields under the hood also do their part to improve the air flow.

The resulting cooling capacity can handle ambient temperatures of up to 122° Fahrenheit at 15 miles per hour—far exceeding requirements in North America or Europe but essential in Australia, and easily handling the cooling needs of 600-hp engines from Caterpillar and Cummins.

The design equally offers help when the engine has to be serviced. An on-road mechanic can reach into a new 50-inch toolbox for his equipment, and then access the transmission, clutch, and back of the engine by removing side panels. The increased space around the engine offers improved access to the fanbelt, exhaust, piping, clutch, and transmission. Still, the shape of the truck is not all function and

no form. The look of the rounded nose can be further enhanced with an optional color-coordinated air dam, full chassis fairings, and side skirts.

Inside, the look has been equally enhanced. Both the dash and the overhead console are available in an optional wood-grained finish as part of a trim kit that includes a soft-touch vinyl dash, gold bezels for VDO gauges, wood inserts for the steering wheel, and leather-trimmed seats. But neither is the inside's form without function. A new overhead console offers access to all electrical switches, air conditioner controls, AM/FM radio and a storage compartment with a door. The truck's engine brake and headlamps are operated with toggle switches, while rocker switches are added for other functions to ensure that they aren't accidentally activated. The space also has room for the engine management system.

Down below is the door for an enlarged glove compartment, while the entire fascia is covered with more gauges than could be found in the T604. The wraparound dash also features drink holders, room for two CB radios, a defrosting outlet for side windows, and an area left for the cellphone. The entire dash is mounted on hinges for access to electrical wiring harnesses that are stored underneath.

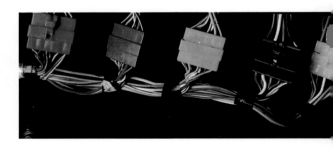

Seats have been moved further apart than those of the T604 to allow more room for a refrigerator and easier access to the sleeper. And the red light that floods the floor below is designed to reduce the tunnel vision that can be associated with night driving. Further enhancing the aerodynamics is a range of integrated sleepers. While the truck is available with traditional modular sleeper boxes—in 36- and 50-inch flat-roof and Aerodyne versions—the T604 is also available with its own integrated sleeper cabs that run on air bag suspensions. The T604 IT incorporates a flat roof and a 28-inch sleeper to meet the particular needs of bulk haulers. For those looking to enhance aerodynamics, the T604 Aero 36 incorporates an Aerodyne roof and 36-inch sleeper compartment, with a recessed back panel that allows for the 32 pallet B-double capacity needed in Australia. And at the top of the line is the T604 Aero 50 that offers full-standing headroom, additional storage, hanging closet space, an optional TV and VCR, and an optional second bunk.

THE T950
A TRADITION OF STYLE

Kenworth Australia makes no apologies for retaining a traditional look for its T950, with an aggressive front end that has made the nameplate a staple in the world's harshest trucking environment. Modeled after the SAR, the truck is designed to operate in virtually any application, from logging to livestock; from a single trailer to a triple road train.

With its distinctive high-mounted cab set back from the engine, more room is left inside the cab and there is more flexibility in the layout of the frame. Batteries, for example, can be located under the cab to leave extra capacity for multiple fuel tanks or a shortened wheelbase. To mount a toolbox under the cabin, batteries are simply mounted to the frame.

The sloped hood, meanwhile, offers a clear view of the road that can be further enhanced with Daylite doors and drop-down windows. Inside, the cab is protected from the heat and noise of the engine with an optional dual-skinned firewall that will duct fresh air past the front of the cabin and underneath the floor.

Sleeper boxes are available for the T950 in 36- and 50-inch sizes, with a standard flat roof or a range of aerodynamic roofs and fairings. With a BBC of 122 inches and an axle setting of 31.9 inches, the flat sleeper has a height that stretches 80.7 inches to the frame. And another 22.8 inches is added with the 36-inch Aero II sleeper, or 23.2 inches with the 50-inch sleeper. In an Aero Roof model there's an additional 29½ to 47½ inches in height.

And for the owner-operator with a sense of style, optional dual exhausts can incorporate names laser cut into the exhaust shields. They add to the look of a traditional style.

MANUFACTURER: Kenworth

TRUCK: T950

BBC: 122 inches

DISTINCTIVE FEATURES: Traditional look with an aggressive front end

PREMIUM SLEEPER: 50-inch Aero II sleeper

THE ROAD TRAIN

RIGHT There are few operating environments as challenging as Australia. Not only does the continent allow some of the longest combinations—road trains—but the high-horsepower engine requirements also face additional cooling requirements because of high ambient temperatures. This is an environment for aggressive-looking front ends and their large radiators.

RIGHT Although road train configurations are suitable for hauling bulk liquids or livestock down the long, straight roads of Australia, they aren't practical in more populated areas such as European cities.

THE K100 G
A CABOVER IN THE LAND OF CONVENTIONALS

The traditional view of an Australian road train places a bonneted rig at the front, grinding its way down desert highways. The K100G cabover, however, is a solution for those who need to find added length.

Where length is particularly important and a sleeper isn't needed, it's available in a 66.9-inch size for better maneuverability and a maximum trailer length. When the sleeper is needed, however, it can be ordered in a 90½-inch length that's suitable for a B-double operation, and a 114-inch model for those who are looking for yet more room. (The K100G 90½-inch Aerodyne is perfectly suited for B-triple applications, with advanced fiberglass and aluminum construction that result in a low tare weight and maximum strength.)

An extensive use of aluminum and fiberglass helps limit the truck's tare weight, allowing a gross mass payload limit exceeding 77 tons with B-triple tri-axle trailers. And with the cabover design, two more pallets can be accommodated within the 110-foot limit without skimping on sleeper space.

MANUFACTURER: Kenworth

TRUCK: K100G

DISTINCTIVE FEATURES: Extensive use of aluminum and fiberglass designed to limit the truck's tare weight

PREMIUM SLEEPER: 114 inches

LEFT Several options enhance the cab, including (1) a pepper window, (2) button tucked interior, (3) dash with woodgrain inserts and, of course (4) radio contact with the outside world.

BELOW A cabover design means that two more pallets can fit iinto maximum 100-foot lengths, while not sacrificing space in the sleeper.

The truck, available in both flat-roof and Aerodyne versions, can also be equipped with optional twin-steer axles that can be ordered to move more weight to the front of the truck—which is particularly ideal in heavy-duty haulage, logging, or mining applications. And the flat roof doesn't have to mean an end to aerodynamics, with an optional roof-mounted spoiler, side skirts, and a wheel arch panel.

Bowing to the fact that cabover designs are more difficult to enter than their conventional counterparts, grab handles surround the door, with access steps cut into both sides of the cab.

Four-way mirrors add to the view of the deep windshield, which can be coupled with Daylite doors and optional peeper windows. But to help keep more elements outside, the engine tunnel is also fitted with a high-density foam insulation that keeps out both heat and noise from the engine compartment.

BELOW The 90-½-inch Aerodyne is well-suited for B-triple operations.

LEFT A flat roof can be special as a way to control costs, when aerodynamics aren't as much of an issue.

MACK TRUCKS
ALLENTOWN, PENNSYLVANIA

Even outside of the trucking industry, the Mack Trucks name has pushed into popular culture. "Built like a Mack truck" is a phrase synonymous with all things robust. But its roots aren't in the trucking industry at all. The truck builder with a long history in Allentown, Pennsylvania, saw its beginnings in Brooklyn, New York, when Augustus and Jack Mack purchased the Fellesen Wagon Factory in 1893. (Their brother William was brought in as a partner.)

Mack didn't actually consider building motorized vehicles until 1901, when Jack took a ride in his first horseless carriage. But he saw them as the future of their business. And while the Mack name is synonymous with trucks, its first commercial vehicle was in fact the Manhattan sightseeing bus that plied the streets around Prospect Park. Trucks didn't come about until 1905, when the Senior line was launched. And in 1906, the company moved to its present home in Allentown, Pennsylvania.

It was supervising engineer John Calder, however, who was responsible for turning Mack to the conventional truck style that would make the company famous, even as most North American makers focused on COE designs. He was influenced by the European stylings of Renault and its upward-sloped hoods.

While still true to its North American roots, Mack's links to Europe haven't been forgotten, either. It's now owned by Renault VI.

ABOVE The CH Series was to be joined in 1999 by a new cab specifically designed for line-haul applications.

BELOW A gold bulldog on the head signifies a Mack powertrain. Other models are signified by a silver mascot.

THE CH SERIES
THE BULLDOG FOR A MODERN ERA

The CH603 is available with set-back or set-forward axles.

It is, perhaps, the best-known mascot in the trucking industry. But the bulldog mounted on the hood of the CH Series or any other Mack truck is also a telling indicator of its power. While every Mack is adorned with a silver version of the bulldog, a gold-colored version indicates a Mack powertrain underneath. And Mack is one of the few North American manufacturers to offer a proprietary powertrain from the engine to the transmission. The bulldog, however, is only the final touch for the CH Series of trucks.

The CH602, a 4 x 2 tractor with a maximum gross combination weight of 140,000 pounds and the CH603 6 x 4 tractor with its 240,000-pound GCW, are both available with set-back or set-forward axles in a 112-inch BBC design.

With seven sleeper-box configurations, the CH Series' homes for truckers include the eight-foot-tall, 74-inch Mack Millennium Sleeper, as well as 42-, 50-, and 60-inch boxes. Wrapped in a covering of chrome and customized colors, the top-sized

MANUFACTURER: Mack

TRUCK: CH603

BBC: 112 inches

DISTINCTIVE FEATURES: The all-seeing bulldog hood ornament that sits atop every Mack

PREMIUM SLEEPER: 74-inch Millennium

Millennium offers 340 cubic feet of room with 45 cubic feet of cargo space—such as an under-bunk cargo bin—and the ability to store 125 pounds of cargo overhead. Mattresses include 39 x 80-inch Serta designs, while a desktop pulls out to offer added work space for the office on the road.

The 64-inch sleeper design is offered in high-rise, mid-rise, and flat-top configurations, each of which was designed for a specific application. The high rise offers room for two bunks, and is also available with one 48-inch-wide Serta mattress. Mid-rise versions can fit the needs of budget-conscious buyers, while the flat top maintains the same sleeper depth, with the lower roof preferred by grain, bulk, and flatbed haulers. And those dealing with strict length laws can order the 42-inch flat-top sleeper. But roof fairings can still be added to flat tops for aerodynamic-conscious line-haul applications. Throughout, the sleeper's temperature is maintained with the placement of five vents. Outer surfaces, meanwhile, are fastened from

MACK TRUCKS
The Image of the Bulldog

The bulldog mascot that sits atop the hood of every Mack truck was crafted in 1932 in a design fashioned by chief engineer Alfred Fellows Masury. But Leroy Smith is the man who made it shine.

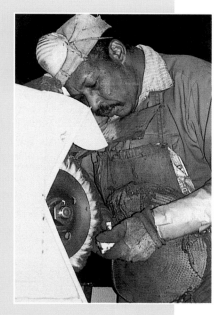

Smith began working for the Victoria Plating Company in Bronx, New York, in 1965, and made a career hand polishing as many as 270 of the hood ornaments each day, about 200 days per year. It's estimated that he polished 1.75 million bulldogs in his 33 years at the plant. "I like work and I like earning money. Getting motivated is easy—I just get up and get going," he said in 1998, preparing for a reluctant retirement. "Whenever I see a Mack, I wonder 'did I polish that dog?'. I feel proud in a way. I like Mack trucks. With that dog, they really look good. If I ever hit the lotto, I'd buy me one truck and just drive it and look at it!"

"He is the hardest-working person I have ever known," said Victoria Plating president Charles Antmann. "He works with tremendous dedication, craftsmanship, and pride."

And he helped keep the image of the bulldog alive.

behind with huckbolts that are hidden from view inside the sleeper. The cab itself is "electrodeposition primed" with a robot-applied base coat/clear coat finish similar to those covering automobiles. Those CH owners who want to round out the look can order an Elite interior package that customizes the cab right down to its woodgrain dash, although four interior packages are available.

Down below, the clutch, brake, and gas pedals have all been positioned for a driver-friendly feel, with a wider gap between the brake pedal and gas pedal to offer improved safety. In the process, repositioned pedals leave more room for the clutch-floating left foot, offering a more comfortable seating position.

But some improvements over previous Mack designs can't be seen. They're found in the weight that isn't there. The AL401LH suspension is 110 pounds lighter than its predecessor, in addition to the 168 pounds shed from the original AL40 design. And

Valeo's integrated radiator/intercooler condensor eliminates 25 pounds when compared to separated units. (Mack was also the first maker of an integrated, charged air-cooling system mounted on the chassis.) Lightweight components added to the product line include aluminum hubs, a redesigned air-ride suspension, and a two-leaf front spring, removing 200 pounds between 1997 and 1998 model years.

Fuel efficiency, though, is a function of the shape as well as the weight as the truck pulls liquid gold from 84-gallon fuel tanks. The AeroPlus aerodynamics package features full chassis fairings and aerodynamic mirrors, in addition to a bumper air dam that, combined, improve aerodynamics by up to 13 percent.

Mack's frames, side rails, crossmembers, and cabs are all covered with a 500,000-mile, five-year warranty. After all, they're built like Mack trucks.

THE MACK POWERTRAIN
Brain, Brawn and Balance

Mack calls its proprietary powertrain nothing less than the Pedigreed. At its heart is the E-Tech electronic engine, which offers between 250 and 454 hp and the V-MAC III electronics system that includes drive-by-wire controls, a list of communication, diagnostic, security, and control features, and a built-in trip recorder.

But the proprietary power doesn't end there. Engine information is sent to drivers through the Co-Pilot display monitor, while built-in self-diagnostics add to the warnings that can be flashed through the dash. The T200 transmission offers three countershafts instead of two, spreading out the load to reduce stress. And the same line includes an aluminum housing for less weight and better heat dissipation. (It's available in configurations of five to 10 speeds, as well as 13 and 18 speeds.)

The top-mounted dual reduction bogie is also meant to reduce stress in the carrier, providing a straight-through driveline that helps reduce the angles that can lead to U-joint wear. Meanwhile, the Mack camelback air suspension forms a parallelogram between the axles, and a full-time cam-and-plunger interaxle differential offers more torque for the driving axle.

LEFT Attention to detail in the Millennium sleeper is apparent in the stitching on the back wall.

MACK TRUCKS AUSTRALIA
THE QUANTUM
A CABOVER FOR THE LAND DOWN UNDER

The Quantum cabover filled the void left in 1997 when Mack Trucks Australia phased out its MHR Ultra-Liner range of trucks. But while this latest bulldog with a flat nose builds largely on the cab of Europe's Renault VI Premium, it draws from a different power source than the standard 11-liter RVI engine traditionally found with the truck. The Quantum's strength is offered by Mack's 12-liter EA7-425 V-MAC II engine with its six cylinders and offerings of 425 hp at 1,800 rpm and peak torque of 1,560 lb-ft at 1,250 rpm. The standard transmission is the Eaton RTLO-16713A 13-speed overdrive design, while an Eaton Valeo single-plate hydraulically actuated clutch and a Spicer 1810HD drive shaft handle the power. The final drive is offered through the Eaton DS 454 P single reduction hypoid drive. When it comes time to slow heavy configurations, a 250-bhp Jacobs engine brake can be further enhanced with a Mack Stealth retarding system to boost stopping power to 320 bhp.

ABOVE The Quantum replaces the MHR, which was phased out of production in 1997.

MANUFACTURER: Mack Trucks Australia

TRUCK: Quantum

BBC: 88 inches

DISTINCTIVE FEATURES: Cabover building on the Renault Premium

PREMIUM SLEEPER: H800 highway sleeper cab

THE MACK-SI INTEGRATED SLEEPER CAB
An Australian flair for North America's CH

The Mack CH range of trucks takes on an Australian flair with the Mack-Si Cab Integrated Sleeper. In Australia, bigger is always better; adding 31 inches to the normal CH cab, this design eliminates the wall between the driver and the sleeper berth. While the sleeper option is about the same size as the 36-inch Lo-Rise Value design, the final result is 220 pounds lighter and six inches shorter from the bumper to the back of the cab.

The size is particularly important with allowances for 48-foot trailers in the Australian market. Amenities include a durable vinyl interior trim, dual reading lights and air vents, under-bunk storage accessed through two doors, a clothes storage area, a drink holder, and a tray to hold personal effects. An optional pleated velour trim is available in grey or crimson colors. The design's aerodynamics can be further improved with the addition of an aerodynamic roof deflector, 165-inch exhaust and air intake snorkel.

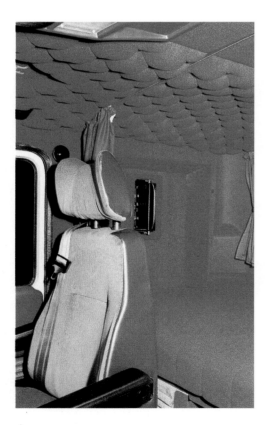

Up above, the Quantum's H800 Highway Sleeper Cab incorporates steel panels strengthened with IFHR steel in high-stress areas. And its interior is accessed through doors that open 90 degrees, unveiling a Deluxe interior trim with a grey plastic fascia. In the midst of the steering column are controls for the Blaupunkt R2448RC stereo. Light filters through a manual sunroof to unveil the sleeper and a 78 x 32 inch inner-spring mattress, which also uses hydraulic ram supports to ease the access to storage areas underneath. Above the bunk is a pouch mounted on the rear wall, along with two independent sleeper lights. Where the sun is let in through the sunroof, a complete cab curtain will block it out.

Other standard features include electrically adjustable mirrors, air conditioning, and four-point cab air suspension. The steering wheel can be adjusted pneumatically, while servicing is eased with the grouping of filler points for everything from windshield washers to air conditioning. With the electrical contacts under the front grille, the cab doesn't have to be tilted for some electrical work. (Although if necessary it will open 60 degrees.)

The rear suspension is a Hendrickson two-bag-per-axle design with a 40,000-pound capacity, and there's an axle spacing of 52 inches. With its 157-inch wheelbase and BBC of 88 inches, the Quantum measures in with a rear overhang of 56 inches. At the front end of the truck is another European influence seen in the Renault E81, 15,655-pound I-beam front axle with Knorr ventilated disc brakes mounted on two parabolic leaf springs. The 80-inch long spring length is fitted with telescopic shock absorbers and a sway bar. Rear braking is offered through the Eaton ES 16.5 x 7-inch drum brakes, and all of it rolls on standard 22.5 x 8.25-inch silver steel disc wheels.

In the end, the truck weighs in with a tare weight of 17,176 pounds with all fluids and 52 gallons of fuel, and offers a gradeability of 41 percent and startability of 20.6 percent. The 158-inch wheelbase and 31-inch sleeper cab can make room for maximum fuel storage space including one 141.7-gallon tank, and a 105.3-gallon fuel capacity. When it's time to round out the aerodynamics, there's an optional roof deflector, 165-inch exhaust and air intake snorkel.

THE TRIDENT ELITE HIGHWAY
BUILT FOR THE SIZE OF THE FUTURE

The Mack Trident was built for Australia, not only to replace the CLR but to offer a flexible design that could meet future length and axle spacing regulations on the island continent.

The Trident's set-forward axle not only allows 520 gallons of fuel storage without overloading the steer axle, but it still caters to the axle spacing requirements for four-axle dog applications, which are mostly used in short-haul environments.

Inside, a grey vinyl trim is accented by a woodgrain dashboard that holds the main instrument panel, with electronic speedometer, odometer, tachometer, and hourmeter. Then there is an array of other gauges including the voltmeter, exhaust pyrometer, engine coolant temperature, air pressure, fuel level, engine oil pressure, brake air application, engine oil temperature, manifold pressure, and transmission and rear axle oil temperature gauges.

The Trident is built around the lightweight CH straight rail chassis, with a huckbolted assembly and low-weight alligator-style crossmembers. Then there's a wide jaw at each end for a wide footprint for frame attachments, increasing lateral stiffness and improving load distribution. It also draws on design features from its

---

MANUFACTURER: Mack Trucks Australia

TRUCK: Trident

BBC: 112 inches

DISTINCTIVE FEATURES: Set-forward axles, built around a CH chassis

PREMIUM SLEEPER: Mack-Si integrated sleeper cab

BELOW The set-forward axle allows additional fuel to be stored for long-distance runs.

Titan brethren: a fully isolated cabin raised six inches higher than the standard CH range to allow for improved visibility and cooling, while dual air intake stacks better filter the air.

The base Elite model is powered by the 470-hp E-Tech EA7 V-MAC III to handle a standard 70-ton Gross Combination Mass.

Although it comes with a standard 174-inch wheelbase, the design is also available with 186-, 193-, 198-, 204-, and 210-inch lengths, as well as a 216-inch design which is capable of handling 442 gallons of fuel, and a larger 224 inches for 520 gallons of fuel.

Available sleepers include the 31.5-inch Mack-Si rear cabin extension, 36-inch Lo-Rise Premium sleeper, 42-inch mid-rise Premium Sleeper and 48-inch mid-rise Prestige sleeper. Its tare weight of 18,436 pounds is coupled with a 112-inch BBC, 9-inch road clearance, GCM of 154,185 pounds and gradeability of 50.54 per cent and startability of 23.76 per cent when coupled with a 93,612-pound GCM.

When it's time to reach underneath, the hood easily opens a full 75 degrees with the assistance of springs. Rounding out the look at the front of the truck and adding the finishing touch are the Bocar bullbars, available in a satin or polished alloy finish.

BELOW A Trident ready to show, shine or drive, complete with polished Bocar bullbars.

THE MACK TITAN
THE BIGGEST BULLDOG OF THEM ALL

Built for extra heavy-duty hauls, the Titan is the largest road-going truck built by Mack Trucks Australia—the biggest bulldog of them all. Capable of Gross Combination Ratings of up to 120 tons, the truck draws from 610 hp produced under the hood, making it a practical choice for B-Doubles, in applications ranging from logging to livestock.

The EA9 610 V-MAC II offers 2,050 lb-ft of torque. While it produces 1,300 Nm of pulling power when the clutch is engaged, and 2,500 Nm at 1,000 rpm, it also delivers 2,508 Nm of torque through more than 80 percent of its operating range.

Incorporating the high swirl injection and V-MAC II electronic controls typical to other Mack engine designs, the EA9 610 is heralded as the most responsive and fuel efficient 16.4-liter V8 ever built by the company. Ultimately, it offers a gradeability of 21 percent when loaded to a 198,207-pound Gross Combination Weight, with a startability of 15 percent. "Whether you're pulling six decks of wild bush Brahman through bulldust in the Top End, pounding over corrugations and wheel ruts on a haul road in the West, or hauling logs over rugged mountain outcrops down South, the Titan XHD will stand the test of time," Mack Australia says.

But with heavy-duty work comes a need for heavy-duty designs. Heavy-duty wiring includes a battery isolation switch, manual reset circuit breakers and fully insulated petroleum wiring. The design's low alloy heat-treated steel frame measures 273 x 83 x 10 mm, carrying two 130-gallon alloy fuel tanks. (It can also be fitted with two 13-inch or four 130-gallon round alloy tanks.) Fitted with a Hayden engine fuel cooler that is mandatory on GCMs of more than 198,207 pounds, the truck also includes polished cab skirts and air intake tubes with PVH dust extractors in front of the external mirrors.

ABOVE With a BBC of 122 inches, Gross Combination Mass Rating of 198,207-pounds, and a ground clearance of 9 inches, the Titan weighs in with a tare weight of 18,939-pounds. It is also available with wheelbases of 217 inches, 227 inches, and 234 inches.

MANUFACTURER: Mack Trucks Australia

TRUCK: Titan

BBC: 122 inches

DISTINCTIVE FEATURES: The largest road-going truck built by Mack Trucks Australia.

THE HIGHWAY RANGE
ON THE ROAD AND DOING THE JOB

ABOVE A light weight helped earn the Fleet-Liner truck-of-the-year honors in 1997.

MANUFACTURER: Mack Trucks Australia

TRUCK: Fleet-Liner

BBC: 112 inches

DISTINCTIVE FEATURES: The lightest heavy-duty design in its market

PREMIUM SLEEPER: 42 inches

Mack Trucks Australia's on-highway range of trucks is a diverse one, but the design that has won many of the accolades is the one that offers the least—the least weight.

The Fleet-Liner was unveiled as the lightest heavy-duty truck in its market, leading to Truck of the Year honors in 1997. It has a tare weight of a mere 15,174 pounds when all fluids are topped up and 52 gallons of diesel fuel fills the tanks. (It comes standard with a pair of 96.3-gallon tanks.) And the truck with a BBC of 112 inches is capable of pulling a 103,508-pound GCMR with a gradeability of 41 percent and startability of 20.9 percent at a GCM of 93,598 pounds.

That's made possible with a 410-hp E-Tech engine backed up with a North American driveline and V-Mac III engine electronics, all of which can be slowed with the help of an incorporated J-Tech engine brake.

The Fleet-Liner has a 169-inch wheelbase with a 56-inch rear overhang, riding on a single frame rail of 258 x 88 x 8-mm low-alloy heat-treated steel. And sitting on that is a galvanized steel cab that incorporates steel doors and a sheet-molded-compound hood and fenders with splash aprons. The look is accented by a silver-painted grille, chrome headlight bezels, and an external sun visor.

Inside, standard instrument gauges are limited to speedometer, odometer, tachometer, hourmeter, with a voltmeter, exhaust pyrometer, engine coolant temperature, air pressure, fuel level, and engine oil pressure gauges. But a Premium Pack includes the addition of engine oil temperature, manifold pressure, transmission oil temperature, brake air application, and rear axle oil temperature dials. A chrome grille and five roof-mounted amber marker lights round off the lock.

A Benchmark Plus interior can introduce woodgrain into the main instrument panel that is usually fitted with a simple black fascia. And there's the potential

addition of an air restriction gauge, spotter windows, and a power passenger window.

The driver oversees it all on a KAB 554B air ride seat behind an 18-inch adjustable steering wheel, while the passenger sits on a fixed cushion design.

The view outside is kept clear with the help of heated mirrors supported with stainless steel arms and brackets, while a variable-speed windshield wiper draws on a reservoir mounted under the hood.

Sleepers are available in a 31.5-inch Mack-Si Cab, 36-inch three-door Lo-Rise Value sleeper, and 42-inch four-door Lo-Rise Value sleeper model. And the overall design is available in wheelbases of 186, 193, 198, 204, 210, and 218 inches.

It's all built to go the distance with fuel stored in two 132.6-gallon or two 93.6-gallon alloy tanks. The Select design, meanwhile, is powered by a 435-hp E-tech engine or an optional 470-hp E-tech powerplant. But the Value-Liner is built for the budget-conscious operator, powered with a 370-hp E-Tech engine. Its tare weight of 15,1738 pounds is coupled with a BBC of 112 inches and GCM of 103,508 pounds, with a gradeability of 37.52 percent and startability of 19.16 percent with a 93,598-pound GCMR.

This design is available with the Mack-Si cab rear cabin extension on the Benchmark Plus interior, or the 36-inch Lo-Rise Value sleeper. When aerodynamics are key, there's a roof fairing and cab extension panels, with a 165-inch exhaust and air intake snorkel on the 36-inch Lo-rise models. They're all built for business.

ABOVE A Fleet-Liner sits ready for the open highway, leading a tridem trailer combination.

BELOW Gleaming specifications can be found right down to the polished fuel tanks.

MAN Nutzfahrzeuge AG
Germany

MAN may have begun its corporate life building steam engines, but it was the work with a man who created a self-named engine that brought diesel power to the world in 1892.

The company worked in conjunction with inventor Rudolf Diesel to build the world's first diesel engines at two plants found in the cities appearing in the company's full name: Maschinenfabrik Augsburg-Nurnberg. But the first design was a stationary one. MAN didn't make a commercial vehicle until 1915—two years after Diesel's death—and it turned to gasoline engines for the power.

The company's first truck was a four-tonner powered by a 36-hp engine and chain drive, and was produced under a Saurer licence in a plant MAN took over at Lindau on Lake Constance.

MAN didn't abandon its early ties to diesel power; a 45-hp model that was unveiled in 1923 incorporated a direct-injected diesel design that was the first of its kind in the world. MAN set up a plant in Munich, Germany in 1955 and in 1971 acquired the Bussing motor vehicle company. Today its truck line spans from six to 48 tons, covering light, medium, and heavy model ranges.

The MAN Commercial Vehicles Subgroup was formed in 1991 with the merging with Austrian-based OAF-Graf and Stift, and Steyr Nutzfahrzeuge.

MAN: THE F2000
THE FUEL SAVER

MAN set out to prove a point with its EcoChallenge Tour of 1995, taking a 1,740 mile run between Edinburgh, Scotland and Bari, Italy with its F2000 designs. And the point was made with a record fuel economy of 25.2 liters per 61 miles achieved by a truck laden with a 40-ton semitrailer train and a 13-foot body height. (Granted, the trucks were specially equipped and had particularly skilled drivers at the helm.)

The focus on fuel economy is quite a contrast considering that MAN technology also powers Super Truck racers in Europe, where it groups four-valve engines with two turbochargers to increase the power of 12-liter, in-line six-cylinder designs. The radiator, intercooler, and electronically controlled injection system for that power come from MAN's yacht engine line, and the resulting designs offer 1,000 hp from 1,800 to 2,600 rpm.

But those trucks are for the track. The F2000 was designed with the needs of an on-highway truck in Europe. And the on-highway needs and wants are changing—right down to the desired looks of a truck. The radiator grille typical to MAN F2000s was recently redesigned without a frame. And deflectors have been pushed higher to form a line with the front flap to keep side windows and rear-view mirrors clear of dirt.

With the exception of the 600-hp super engine, F2000 Euro2 turbocharged engines are in-line six-cylinder electronically managed models. And long-haul operations are further eased with the incorporation of direct-drive transmissions from Eaton and ZF for use with 360, 410, and 460-hp engines. The gears, meanwhile, are shifted with the help of compressed air and the Servoshift.

MANUFACTURER: MAN

TRUCK: F2000

DISTINCTIVE FEATURES: Design built with a focus on fuel economy

PREMIUM SLEEPER: FB cab

BELOW From road racing teams to typical roads of freight, the F2000 is built to haul an array of loads.

The truck range is designed to stay on the road. All of its engines, gearboxes, and axles are supplied with synthetic lubricants, incorporating enlarged oil volumes to extend engine oil change intervals to 50,000 miles, with gearbox and axle oils lasting 190,000 miles. A recently introduced single-cylinder air compressor with a 22-cubic-inch displacement feeds 380 liters of air per minute, and loses less power than the two-cylinder design that preceded it.

When weight is a concern, operators can collect up to 880 pounds of extra payload with an F2000 through the specifications of aluminum rims, compressed air reservoirs and tanks; by removing the spare wheel; incorporating only a single bunk in the cab; and removing the co-driver's seat.

The F sleeper cabs are mounted on a four-point cab suspension and can tilt 60 degrees, while they are held in place with an automatic double-locking mechanism. And an underbumper air dam improves aerodynamics with quarter panel air deflectors. Illuminated entry steps lead the way to the interior and an air-cushioned driver's seat fitted with a headrest and seatbelt, with storage pockets fitted into the door. The view from the seat is helped with rear view, wide angle, and curb-view mirrors that are all heated and electrically controlled.

An expanded design is offered in the FB cab with its tinted glass, external sun visor, headlight washer system, and a six-speaker sound system. An automatic electronic two-man tachograph takes its place along with a rev counter, additional gauges, and warning lights, and the ride is managed with cruise control, while an

automatic chassis lubrication feature keeps the components seizure-free. The F and FB sleepers both sit over 141-inch wheelbases with 60-inch front overhangs and 40-inch rear overhangs. With a laden cab height of 37 inches, the truck's turning circle measures 472 inches. And where tare weights for the F sleeper-equipped cabs are available in 13,900-pound (with a 9,600-pound front axle) or 14,000-pound sizes with a 9,700-pound front axle, the FB sleeper weighs in at 14,200 pounds with a 9,700-pound front axle.

But don't expect to see many of these trucks sitting in the filling stations. One of the goals in Europe is to develop a vehicle that doesn't have to be refueled between destinations, which has led to the addition of aluminum fuel tanks with 104 or 202.8 gallons of volume. With 312 gallons of diesel in two tanks, the truck can travel 2,235 miles without having to stop.

ABOVE F and FB sleepers both sit over 141-inch wheelbases.

NAVISTAR INTERNATIONAL
CHICAGO, ILLINOIS

Navistar International trucks will have a tough time shedding their nicknames of "cornbinder" and "cornhusker" on the CB. The company's rich roots in the farming industry cannot be denied.

In 1831, the company was born when Cyrus Hall McCormick built his first grain reaper. And by the turn of the century, in 1902, the McCormick family, William Deering, and several other makers of farm machinery convinced J.P. Morgan and Co. to underwrite the International Harvester Co. for $120 million.

By 1907, the new company was making "Auto Buggy" passenger cars. And the Auto Wagon Express—designed to haul farm produce—was unveiled in 1909 as the company's first truck, with an 84-inch wheelbase.

Today, Navistar International is firmly entrenched as one of North America's leading truck manufacturers, building medium and heavy trucks as well as school buses, mid-range diesel engines, and all-makes parts.

BELOW The 9000 Series is far removed from the just-for-work farm machinery built by Cyrus Hall McCormick in the 1800s.

THE 9000-SERIES
EAGLES FOR THE OPEN ROAD

The top-of-the-line trim package for International's 9000 Series of trucks carries a truly American symbol of freedom: the Eagle. And indeed, these Eagles have a distinctive look on the open road. A stainless-steel grille surround forms a backdrop for the diamond-shaped logo that graces the nose of each truck. And inside, the VIP steering wheel is a luxurious addition to dual armrests and a diamond-button-tucked soft trim on the walls.

But the profile of every 9000 Series truck is distinctive it its own right. Standard aluminum bumpers and swept-back fenders finish off the look of a cab that's protected by a multilayer finish. Its high-concentration color coat is sealed with a clear urethane. Up front, the three-piece center-point-mounted hood is formed with a computerized sheet-molded compound process for a better fit and finish. Meanwhile, the hood-assist springs and a hood-dampening hydraulic shock absorber make it easier to open and close. And integrated splash panels are designed for easier engine access once the aerodynamic nose is lifted out of the way.

Inside the cab, the wraparound instrument panel features gauges set into a burled woodgrain background, with chrome bezels wrapping around their edges. The driver and passenger seats can even swing around 180 degrees to double as easy chairs for the sleeper. But when it's time to work, the driver's seat slides back and forth by nine inches to offer more legroom. And there's 23 inches of space between the seats.

Lighting is offered by two overhead dome lights, two door-mounted courtesy lights, and a reading light above each door that can offer full or spot illumination.

Storage is key on the road, and such space is available in a number of areas. A flapped map pouch on the

BELOW With a 120-inch BBC, the 9400 Eagle is the flagship of Navistar's Class 8 premium conventionals.

driver's-side door is complemented by a netted storage compartment above the driver. The closets in the sleeper feature slotted clothes rods to keep hangers from sliding around while the truck moves down the highway.

When it's time to sleep, a 37-inch-wide mattress is standard for the lower bunk, although a 53-inch version is available in the 72-inch-long Pro Sleeper design. And in terms of the look, interior Eagle colors are available in five vinyl or cloth options, while an additional premium color series is available in vinyl.

With a 120-inch BBC, the 9400 is a flagship in International's 9000 Series, with a hood optimized to handle 12- or 14-liter power plants. Built around 10 to 12 liters of power, the 9200's 112-inch BBC design is built for tighter spaces, with an improved line of sight and a lighter chassis.

Those wanting to customize the look of the long-nosed 9300 Eagle can choose from a variety of options, including dual cowl-mounted, 11-inch steel air cleaners. These can be further customized with a stainless-steel air deflector fitted over the elbow. Then there is a stainless-steel sunshade, a full-depth and chromed-aluminum front bumper, additional running lights, and polished fuel tanks.

In every truck, long-stroke brake chambers are standard, as are daytime running lights. But when it's time to order one of these trucks, the process is also easier than ever. The 9000 Series can be ordered using Diamond Spec, which prepackages 200 different option groups using thousands of different vehicle combinations in 11 categories. And when International can prepick the parts, the warranty coverage is doubled to two years or 200,000 miles, there's the availability of a replacement truck if a repair can't be made in 24 hours, and there's an emergency breakdown service and prepackaged extended warranties. As International says, "We take pride in your ride."

THE 9800
OUT OF THE DOGHOUSE

The first thing you notice about International's 9800 cabover is something that's missing. The doghouse—the annoying engine tunnel traditional to COE designs—is gone. And it's only five inches high when coupled with the high horsepower of a Cummins N14 or Detroit Diesel Series 60 engine. As the first North American truck maker to create a flat-floor cabover, International won the Truck Writers of North America's technical achievement award. But improvements to the design weren't limited to flattening the floor. The ergonomic shift lever, for example, was moved toward the instrument panel. Large white-on-black gauges feature wide-sweeping angles that help draw attention to small changes in operating conditions. And a center-mounted convenience console offers three divided spaces with room for a mug, paperwork, and a satellite system keyboard.

Aerodynamics are improved with a 12½-inch front corner radius that stretches from the windshield to the bumper, and a 25⅜-inch-tall windshield that slopes 15 degrees. When it's time to clean the two pieces of the windshield that aren't reached by 20-inch wiper blades, drivers have the added benefit of a front grab handle.

The truck has a 53½-inch setback axle and a 40-degree wheel cut, while a set-forward model offers an option for those buyers who face special weight requirements. The 9800's overall weight is controlled with an all-aluminum cab—there's no steel used in its construction. Even the roof is made of stamped

MANUFACTURER:	Navistar International
TRUCK:	9800
BBC:	89, 110 inches
DISTINCTIVE FEATURES:	Flat-floored interior
PREMIUM SLEEPER:	110-inch Hi-Rise

BELOW While Navistar announced in 1998 that it would no longer build cabover designs in North America, production was moved to Mexico to meet the needs of export markets.

aluminum that's welded into place. The cab and its doors—which measure 56³/₁₆ x 35³/₁₆ inches—are constructed with riveted and bonded skins to reduce the potential of leaks and corrosion. Door windows add to the outside view with their 20¹/₁₆ x 20¹/₄-inch openings.

The cab even manages to keep some elements outside when the door or window is open, with a drip rail around the cab designed to ensure that water doesn't rush in. Inside, there's 61 inches of room from the back of the seat to the back of the cab. And there's more than 90 inches of headroom in Hi-Rise versions, with five feet of upward space in flat-roof configurations. With sleepers, the 9800 is available as an 89-inch and 110-inch flat-roof, or a 110-inch Hi-Rise design.

The mounting of parts offers its own improvements. Dual air tanks are protected below frame rails, just inboard of the fuel tanks. The transmission oil cooler mounted on the radiator is more efficient than designs mounted under the chassis because of the bonus of forced air and added protection. The cab doesn't even have to be raised to reach the power-steering reservoir that's mounted on the frame behind the cab. The surge tank, too, is mounted on top.

The 9800's fuse panel offers space for 56 breakers and 25 relays, and it can be opened without tools in less than 10 seconds, with the panel mounted at a 25-degree incline for easier access.

The airflow in the wide-open design is boosted through 64¹/₃ square inches of salem vents that measure 12¹/₄ x 5¹/₄ inches. Crank-out awning-style vent windows add to the environment, and there are three heating, ventilation, and air-conditioning outlets in the sleeper. (A remote control panel is mounted on the wall at the head of the bunk.) When it's time to sleep, a vinyl bunk curtain slides along its rail and closes with the help of magnets. And for those needing more bed space, a 53-inch-wide mattress is available in the 110-inch design. A 28-inch bunk comes as standard in the upper position of the Hi-Rise.

There's even room for a TV and a 14-inch-wide hanging closet in 110-inch BBC configurations that include flat-roof and Hi-Rise designs. Electrical accessories can be easily added thanks to a 12-volt power outlet in the sleeper. And there's no need to fumble with keys to open the outside luggage compartment that incorporates cable controls.

The designers obviously kept their feet planted firmly—and flat—on the floor.

THE 9900 EAGLE
AN EAGLE FOR THE OWNER-OPERATOR

Navistar International makes no secret about focusing on the fleet market, but the Eagle 9900 was unveiled in 1998 with the owner-operator in mind.

Sporting a wider grille and longer hood, the chrome-rimmed headlamps add to the aggressive look of a long-nosed conventional design that had been returning to popularity for more than five years. International met with 100 truck drivers and fleet managers with no more than 10 trucks, showing them various designs, and asked their opinion on length and style of hoods, frame rails, sideview mirrors, BBC dimensions, set-forward axles, and fuel tanks. The final result: a 6 x 4 tractor with a 120-inch bumper-to-back-of-cab dimension and a set-forward front axle.

For show, the look is rounded out with external air cleaners and a dual-mounted cab exhaust, and for power, this is also the first International to incorporate a 600-hp engine. It also shares a common chassis with the 9200 and 9400 conventional designs. And by incorporating new Owens Corning insulation like its brethren, the cab is designed to be comfortable in -20.2° Fahrenheit without the use of an auxiliary heater. Both door handles have a draft barrier, while improvements were made to the sidewalls, roof, floor, luggage compartment, roof-to-cab interface, and cab-to-trim contact surfaces to keep the elements shut out.

MANUFACTURER: Navistar International

TRUCK: 9900

BBC: 120 inches

DISTINCTIVE FEATURES: Aggressive look, long-nosed conventional design

PREMIUM SLEEPER: 72-inch Sky-Rise Pro Sleeper

THE SKY-RISE
Reaching up for Added Space

Marketed as the most spacious sleeper on the road, International's Sky-Rise features a 102-inch-high ceiling coupled with the room of a 72-inch-long Pro-Sleeper design. Traditionally, the size of a sleeper is referred to more in terms of its length and width. But with the added height, driver teams can enjoy 35 inches of space between the bunks, and there's even room to sit on the top bunk.

The height eliminates the need for an air fairing to improve aerodynamics. The roof itself offers the aerodynamic sculpting, and can shave 50 pounds from the weight of a sleeper because there's no need for the roof-shaping addition.

The Hi-Rise design also offers added storage space that includes a standard shelf above the windshield.

Since it has more than its share of space to fill, a new heating, ventilation, and air-conditioning system was designed.

Its smaller cousin, the Hi-Rise Pro Sleeper is available in 51- and 72-inch lengths, and includes a wraparound storage area with room for a TV and VCR, a microwave, and refrigerator. A pull-out desk adds to the list of amenities.

LEFT The long-nosed conventional marked an aggressive look for North American owner-operators, with a design that is capable of handling high-horsepower engines.

PETERBILT MOTORS COMPANY
DENTON, TEXAS

rucks built by the Fageol Truck and Coach Company always carried the informal moniker of "Bill-Bilt" as homage to its president, W.H. Bill. That's why Alfred (Al) Peterman chose the name Peterbilt when he bought the Oakland, California, manufacturer in 1939.

Peterman's primary interest may have been in building chain-driven logging trucks for his lumber operations in Tacoma, Washington State, but the appeal of Peterbilts stretched well beyond his company. (Still, the manufacturing operation focused on quality instead of quantity. It only built 82 units in 1940.) In fact, Peterbilt's Western roots played a significant role in the truck line's development, given that its strength and reputation were built under the more liberal weight laws found on the West Coast. It's here that its trademark long-nose conventional was born.

The company was sold in 1958 to the Pacific Car and Foundry—which owned Kenworth—but Peterbilt has also held true to its traditions. While its fellow PACCAR company is known for radical changes in truck designs, the most successful Peterbilt models continue to offer the long-nosed styling that has made them a mainstay of North America's trucking industry.

BELOW The Peterbilt name is synonymous with the classic look of a long-nosed conventional truck.

MODEL 379
A LEGENDARY LOOK ON THE INTERSTATE

Peterbilt promotes its Model 379 as no less than a legend, and truck buyers have responded by making it the company's best-selling truck of all time. With its classic long-nose conventional styling, this truck offers the quintessential image of a long-nosed "Pete" with an optional 119- or 127-inch elongated aluminum hood. Where the hood conveys power, it also holds it. The Model 379 can be ordered with engines of up to 600 hp, not to mention a variety of suspensions including proprietary designs that incorporate lightweight aluminum components.

The cabs, too, make an extensive use of aluminum alloys, offering a lighter weight than steel. And the roof itself is seamless, dealing with the threat of leaks. Sometimes weight isn't the only concern, however. Those working in tough on/off-road applications can select tougher frame rails, crossmembers, and drivetrains. Aircraft-grade huckbolts are used instead of rivets to fasten panels in place, offering six times the strength of traditional fasteners. And when it comes time for maintenance, the massive hood tilts 90 degrees for easy engine access.

The truck's frame is built with $10^{5/8}$ x $^{5/16}$-inch steel rails, steel crossmembers, and gussets. And a 12,000-pound front axle and 40,000-pound rear axle by Eaton are also standard. For the sake of comfort, a Unibilt sleeper secures the cab and sleeper together in a single unit, offering more room in the home away from home. The layout of the interior, meanwhile, was designed by a computer analysis, while "Pete's"

MANUFACTURER: Peterbilt

TRUCK: Model 379

DISTINCTIVE FEATURES: Traditional long-nosed conventional design

PREMIUM SLEEPER: Ultra Sleeper

customers helped determine such things as the best position for the seat and layout of the instruments.

Premium-finish aluminum alloys are used for the standard fuel tank, offering a gleaming surface. But from a practical standpoint, it also features a dual-draw/dual-return fuel system with a tank equalization valve.

Even square-nosed conventionals have to be conscious of aerodynamics in some applications, so roof fairings, side trim tabs, and cab extenders allow the truck to be customized for long-haul designs.

For the sake of the look, a stainless steel windshield visor, air cleaner, and polished tool and battery boxes are also available. A stainless-steel radiator grille, traditional polished aluminum radiator surround, aluminum headlamp pods, and polished aluminum bumper can all add to the air of confidence undoubtedly displayed by the driver at the wheel.

MODEL 378
THE BEST OF BOTH WORLDS

ABOVE Padded walls and trim add to the luxury appointments in a Peterbilt sleeper.

The Peterbilt 378 offers the best of two worlds: the agility of an intracity truck, and the horsepower, comfort, and aerodynamics of a long-haul highway tractor.

When it comes to specifications, there are three different cab and axle configurations from which to choose. The 119-inch BBC 378 can be ordered with a set-forward 30-inch axle setting or a 47-inch setback front axle to allow for bigger payloads. And it is also available with the Unibilt Cab Sleeper System, UltraCab Sleeper, UltraSleeper, or Unibilt Day Cab.

In terms of the aerodynamic improvements needed in a long-haul tractor, its full aerodynamics package includes cab extenders and a proprietary roof fairing, while the setback front axle version even features a contour-molded aerodynamic bumper. The hood will tilt 90 degrees for easy engine access, while halogen headlamps are mounted on the grille surround to light the way. Maintenance is further eased with outboard-mounted brake drums. Any of the gauges can snap in and out of place for quick replacement. And a mere four bolts allow the wiper motor to be released from its mounting.

Sometimes, however, the best maintenance-related improvements are those that prevent the work in the first place. Sealed spring pins and bushings in the front suspension reduce maintenance while extending service life. And O-ring connectors protect the wiring from dirt and corrosion. After all, Peterbilt "bilt" it to stay on the road, whatever is thrown at them.

RIGHT For Interstate driving, a 30-inch set-forward axle is fine. A 47-inch setback front axle will allow for bigger payloads.

MANUFACTURER: Peterbilt

TRUCK: Model 378

BBC: 119 inches

DISTINCTIVE FEATURES: Set-forward or set-back axles under a long hood

PREMIUM SLEEPER: Ultra Sleeper

MODEL 377 A/E
A TRUCK SCULPTED FOR THE WIND

The long, square nose of a Peterbilt isn't often considered in terms of aerodynamics, but sculpting was the word of the day with the launch of the Model 377 A/E. The hood of Peterbilt's aerodynamic truck is sloped to reduce drag, as well as increase visibility and form a distinctive profile. Aerodynamics are further improved with a range of roof fairings, trim tabs, and cab side extenders, while a side skirt for the sleeper further lowers wind resistance. And fenders are streamlined with a smoothed outline for the headlamps.

However, not all fuel savings are made by changing a truck's lines. The under-cab fuel tank is available with options that improve weight distribution and increase potential payload.

A setback front axle sharpens the wheel cut to allow this truck to be maneuvered into tighter spaces. Although the 377 A/E is still available in a set-forward axle configuration, with a traditional hood for an improved ride and weight distribution. And again, an all-aluminum cab sheds the weight.

ABOVE Sculpting of the fenders and hood on the Model 377 A/E not only improves on aerodynamics, but it improves visibility.

MANUFACTURER: Peterbilt

TRUCK: Model 377 A/E

DISTINCTIVE FEATURES: Streamlined, aerodynamic design

PREMIUM SLEEPER: Ultra Sleeper

THE ULTRACAB AND ULTRASLEEPER
BILTS WITH SPACE

When Peterbilts are built to offer "ultra" comfort, they include the UltraCab and the Ultra Sleeper.

When compared to other designs, the Unibilt UltraCab includes a 10-inch-taller walkthrough to the sleeper, while the cab roof has been raised five inches to include 63 inches of headroom. That leaves more room for storage in the header area, while the radio is angled directly toward the driver's line of sight. An optional curved one-piece windshield is also available for a more contemporary look, replacing the traditional two-piece windshield.

Several UltraCab features include a dual air bag suspension system, special tracking rod to stabilize the ride, and an extended rear window offering two additional inches of rearward seat travel.

To the rear, the Unibilt UltraCab Sleeper is available on conventional models 379, 377A/E, 385, and 378 in 48- or 63-inch high-roof configurations.

It's the UltraSleeper, however, that offers luxury accommodation. A latching cabinet storage system is offered in addition to directional reading lights, sliding tinted windows with privacy curtains, under-bunk storage with interior access, a refrigerator/freezer mounted at eye level, and sofa-style seating. A lockable baggage

BELOW With the table folded out of the way, there's plenty of room for sofa-style seating.

compartment allows access from both sides of the sleeper's exterior, and a wet locker is optional. An entertainment cabinet and outsize clothes rack rounds out the storage.

But at the top of the line is the addition of a Canadian/American Class interior for added comfort. A full-sized Murphy-style bed folds down to provide an extra-thick mattress and, once it folds up, the space is opened for a large table. Privacy is ensured with the privacy door that pushes out of the way into the extra-length closet. And when you want easy access, you can climb into the sleeper with a passenger-side door.

These are the specifications for "ultra" comfort.

ABOVE For those seeking added comfort, there's the added space of a Peterbilt UltraCab and UltraSleeper.

LEFT A raised roof offers 63 inches of headroom—five inches more than other Peterbilt designs.

BELOW Benefits of an UltraCab design include 10 inches of more height than for the access to the sleeper.

MODEL 362E
THE CABOVER WITH A CONVENTIONAL NAME

MANUFACTURER: Peterbilt

TRUCK: 362E

BBC: 90, 110 inches

DISTINCTIVE FEATURES: Cab-over design

Peterbilt enhanced its premier cabover design with the Model 362E, offering a recontoured profile for a more contemporary look. But looks aren't everything. The sculpting served the purpose of improving aerodynamics. Other fuel-efficient improvements included a swept-back bumper and a lightweight chromed aluminum grille that mimics the styling found on Peterbilt conventionals.

The design is available in a 90- or 110-inch BBC measurement, while the front springs allow the front axle to be set back 35 inches from the bumper for better maneuverability. For easier access, grab handles were also repositioned with the launch of this truck. And the steps are longer and deeper than ever, while the cab itself is five inches lower than its predecessor. For added safety when climbing in and out of the cab at night, steps are illuminated with the turn signal indicator as soon as the door is opened.

But improvements weren't limited to the outside. The doghouse was lowered and the shift lever moved forward for an easier trip to the bunk. And interior packages even include the Classic 3 line that was once only found in conventionals.

Who says a Peterbilt can only have a long nose?

BELOW Who says Peterbilts have to have a profile with a long nose?

RENAULT VI (VEHICULES INDUSTRIELS)
FRANCE

L ouis Renault faced a decision when he returned from military service in September 1898. He could work for his family's textile business or follow his passion for machines with a workshop in his parents' country residence.

He followed his heart. Renault Frères was founded on October 1, 1898, in Billancourt, France (near Paris), only weeks before Renault built his first car to be known as the Voiturette. Even with only six employees, the company managed to build six vehicles. But it was the company's first patent for a direct drive that attracted much of the attention. The 21-year-old inventor had developed a gearbox that used a rigid shaft to transmit power to the rear wheels rather than relying on the chain drive that was common in other designs of the day.

Two years later, Renault Frères created its first delivery van with a 3-hp single-cylinder IC engine positioned under a bench seat and the potential of carrying a 550-pound payload. By 1905 the company had its first one tonners on the market, and a three-ton model powered by a four-cylinder engine was available in 1905.

On January 16, 1945, the company was nationalized to become Régie Nationale des Usines Renault. And three years after Bernard Vernier Palliez took over as chairman in 1975, French truck makers Berliet and Saviem were brought under one umbrella to form the commercial business that is today's Renault VI.

BELOW Renault Frères built its first truck at the turn of the century, while today's Renault VI has a presence around the world.

THE AE MAGNUM
AN INTEGRATED CAB THAT STANDS ALONE

When it was unveiled in 1990, Renault's Magnum turned heads with an integral cab design that sat independently of the drivetrain, towering above the road. Such a design meant an important feature in a cab-over-engine truck. It meant a flat floor in the cab. First launched with 380- and 500-bhp engines, the Magnum has seen numerous improvements. The line was enhanced in 1998 with the Magnum Integrale that drew upon Mack's V-Mac electronics, and the choice of a 12-liter 24-valve engine with ratings of 390, 430, and 470 bhp, and a V8 engine with a rating of 560 bhp. The cab interior was enhanced, while the workings of the truck saw the addition of a new single reduction drive axle and EBS (electronic braking).

The newest versions of the cab can be identified with a black grille that incorporates the bumper, and a horizontal fascia that links the cab to the "technical

ABOVE Mack Trucks indicated that it would bring a version of the Magnum to North America if the cabover market ever expanded on that continent.

MANUFACTURER: Renault VI

TRUCK: AE Magnum

DISTINCTIVE FEATURES: An integral cab design that sits independent of the drivetrain, providing for a flat floor in the interior

PREMIUM SLEEPER: Integrale Cab

LEFT & ABOVE With a cab that sits independent of the drivetrain, Renault was able to provide a maximum amount of space in the AE Magnum's interior (1). With it, there's room for two storage lockers above the windshield (2), a deep storage area under the 78½ x 29½ inch bunk (3), and room in the header for a CB and cellular phone, cleaning up the overall dash (4).

compartment." It's here that you can find the company's signature diamond-shaped emblem. And even the fenders are the same color as the cab.

An eye to ergonomics is apparent throughout the design, with an adjustable steering wheel and wraparound dash. The passenger seat can be pivoted 180 degrees to offer additional seating in the sleeper, but can also be folded in the cab to be converted into a table. The electric controls for the blinds, windows, and defrosters can all be found in the doors, while controls for the radio and cruise control are both grouped on the steering column, with room in the header for a radio-cassette player, CB, or cellular phone. A foldaway writing table is also stored inside the hub of the 18-inch steering wheel. Down below, the accelerator is electronic, offering the same feel as the controls in a private car.

When the day is done, the cab features a main bunk measuring 78¾ x 29½ inches, which can also be used as a sofa thanks to its high position off the floor. A second 74¾ x 27½-inch bunk is also available. An eye has also been given to storage options. There's a bottle carrier on a console to the right of the driver, a 23-liter storage container with room for a bottle inside the door; a compartment for papers at the base of the driver's seat; and two storage lockers above the windshield, with a third to the right of the top bunk. A clothes closet has been fitted behind the passenger seat, and there are three lockers under the lower bunk.

THE PREMIUM
TEAMWORK IN MOTION

The Premium marked more than the introduction of a new truck line in 1996; it marked a new approach to truck making by Renault VI. The truck, veiled under a code name of the H100 project, was developed using a project management team approach that saw employees with a wide range of skills working on the truck as a whole, rather than blinded by the confines of a particular element of the cab. Even suppliers were made full members of the team.

The first cab concepts were presented to managers in 1988. But there were still years of research to be invested into the chassis. The final team was set up in 1992, and in 1993 the truck saw its first styling concepts that gave a true form to the inner and outer shapes. The ultimate design was shaped to find a balance between the lowest possible Cx (drag factor) and the least aggressive shape for the road. Long-haul versions ultimately incorporated a full-height deflector, coupled with an angled windshield.

Drivers access the cab with three steps that lead the way to a door that opens 90 degrees, unveiling the floor of the 98½-inch-wide truck that sits 53 inches above the surface of the road. Inside, the Premium's main bunk measures 86½ x 31½ inches, with an optional second bunk measuring 74¾ x 27½ inches. Of course, comfort isn't only required when a driver is taking a break. Grand Comfort seats are also designed with comfort in mind. And an added feature makes them more functional: the passenger's seat can be folded into a table or simply folded out of the way to ensure more space to move within the cab.

ABOVE The 11.1-liter, 380 hp engine was developed in conjunction with Mack trucks.

MANUFACTURER: Renault

TRUCK: Premium

DISTINCTIVE FEATURES: A lighter design able to carry 600 to 900 kg more payload than previous models

PREMIUM SLEEPER: N/A

BELOW Work on the Premium called for a new manufacturing approach that involved employees working on a team devoted to the truck as a whole, rather than individual elements.

ABOVE Visibility is enhanced with a mirror mounted ahead of the windshield, and a video screen to monitor traditional blindspots.

LEFT With lightweight components, the Premium is capable of carrying 1,300 to 1,400 lb. more payload when compared with previous Renault designs.

BELOW Two seatbelt points are integrated directly into the seats.

And there is room to move. There is 78¾ inches of standing height in the cab that looks onto the road through a windshield sloped at 15 degrees. The view is further enhanced with other additions. A mirror mounted in front of the windshield, for example, offers the driver a view of the road that would normally be blocked by the dash, while a video camera offers full visibility to the rear.

Under the hood is a new 11.1-liter, 380-hp engine developed in conjunction with Mack Trucks. Still weighing 550 to 770 pounds less than a conventional 12-liter engine, the powerplant also incorporates ITC electronic injection, enabling high average speeds, trimming exhaust emissions, and cutting fuel consumption. It can also incorporate the J-type engine brake found in Mack designs.

While the cab will tilt 60 degrees for access to the engine, testing was meant to ensure the longest worry-free life possible. The truck was put to the test at a 40-million-franc test center, helping to prove that the cab's corrosion resistance was increased by 50 percent and resistance to salt mist by 60 percent.

The servicing that is required is eased with the grouping of filler outlets for windshield washer fluid, air conditioning, engine coolant, and electrical contacts. Fuel caps are designed to be filled from a jerrycan without a funnel; battery terminals can be easily accessed; and a special light offers help when changing bulbs.

The truck's overall tare weight was shed by combining as many components as possible, and incorporating a wide use of aluminum, synthetic materials, and high-elastic modulus steel. Overall, there's 1,300 to 1,400 pounds more payload to be had when compared to earlier Renault designs.

There has also been attention afforded to the environment. There are no CFC refrigerants in the air-conditioning system, and the clutch linings don't incorporate asbestos. And even in its final days, a Premium is designed to be a little friendlier to the environment. Almost 92 percent of the truck can be recycled, with plastic components identified for recycling.

THE INTEGRALE CAB
INTEGRAL AND IN A CLASS BY ITSELF
INTEGRAL AND IN A CLASS BY ITSELF

Renault's Integrale cab is built for space. The flat floor is 29-square-feet (excluding the bed), and the interior height is 73½-inches. There's 93 inches from window to window, and from the windshield to the rear panel measures 79½ inches.

But the space isn't limited to the floor. Integrale cabs offer 60,000 cubic inches of storage space including three under-bunk compartments, overhead storage above both doors, and two clothes closets, each of which has a 8,845-cubic-inch storage capacity. And outside, there's access to a 2,104-cubic-inch storage compartment.

Access is easy. Steps behind the axle can be bigger (each measures 16 x 7½ inches). Their nonskid surface won't corrode, and lights have been added. There's also an 8¼ x 27½-inch running board underneath the door, which measures a massive 59 x 37½ inches.

The Integrale's bus-like windshield is made of 31¾ square feet of tinted glass, with another 7¾ square feet of viewing area added through each side window.

The cab itself sits on a low-frequency suspension, filtering out any vibrations exceeding 1 Hz. Mounted on four air springs, three leveling valves keep the cab level at all times, adjusting air pressure to counteract upward or downward motion. The

ABOVE Aerodynamics on the 13-foot-high cab are improved with a roof that forms the shape of a deflector. The Commander passenger seats may sit two inches lower than the driver's seat, but they offer many of the same features.

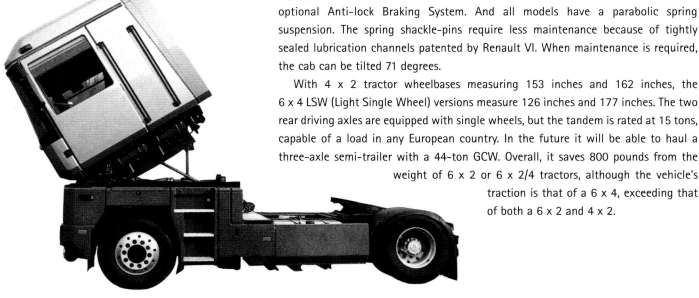

outside elements are further blocked with ½ inch of latex foam carpeting, with another ⅛ inch of ribbed rubber carpeting. In the sleeper, the ¾-inch felt layer on the back panel is further covered with a ½-inch lining. And the side panels are covered with a semi-rigid polyurethane foam lining that's ½ inch thick and meets stringent fire-retarding standards. When insulation isn't enough, internal temperatures are controlled with the Electronic Temperature Management system.

The 18-inch steering wheel incorporates several stalk controls, including lighting, the electrical retarder, and windshield wiper. An in-dash 12-volt outlet that's standard on the Magnum model also incorporates an adjustable mirror that lets drivers shave without leaving the cab. And in terms of power for other accessories, there's wiring for a TV, a refrigerator (standard on the Magnum model), and cellular phones. A hinged table offers room for meals or work.

The Ergovision dashboard is curved and divided into three sections. To the left is the tachograph, electric mirror controls, and controls for the trailer brake. At the steering wheel are main gauges and warning lights. To the right are air and oil pressure gauges, ETM control, spots for the radio, cigar lighter, a 33-warning-light console, and toggle switches. Under the dash is an electrical junction box and a fuse box with independent lighting and a LED fuse tester, and the master circuit breaker.

Commander seats designed for the range offer additional back support. Two seatbelt points are mounted on each seat, with a third on the cab itself.

The cab comes with four or six light sources, with one on each side of the bunk and two overhead lamps on models equipped with an upper bunk. And when light isn't wanted, powered curtains will block out the outside world.

Outside, aerodynamics of the 13-foot-high cab are improved with a roof that forms the shape of a deflector, curved panels beside the grille, and a built-in air dam for the technical module that sits below. Side fairings at the rear of the cab are integrated with the intake used to draw air into the engine. While the cab is built with a treated steel, exposed elements are constructed from an iron/zinc alloy or are coated with PVC.

Air-operated front disc brakes are standard, with drum brakes on the rear axles equipped with automatic slack adjusters, all of which can be specified with an optional Anti-lock Braking System. And all models have a parabolic spring suspension. The spring shackle-pins require less maintenance because of tightly sealed lubrication channels patented by Renault VI. When maintenance is required, the cab can be tilted 71 degrees.

With 4 x 2 tractor wheelbases measuring 153 inches and 162 inches, the 6 x 4 LSW (Light Single Wheel) versions measure 126 inches and 177 inches. The two rear driving axles are equipped with single wheels, but the tandem is rated at 15 tons, capable of a load in any European country. In the future it will be able to haul a three-axle semi-trailer with a 44-ton GCW. Overall, it saves 800 pounds from the weight of 6 x 2 or 6 x 2/4 tractors, although the vehicle's traction is that of a 6 x 4, exceeding that of both a 6 x 2 and 4 x 2.

SCANIA
SWEDEN

In its earliest days, Scania was always on the move. Its first endeavors may have been modest bicycles and motorcycles, but the Swedish company quickly made the jump to automobiles in 1901 with its first passenger car. The first commercial vehicle followed two years later with a two-cylinder, 10-hp Kamper engine mounted under the driver's seat, while a chain drive turned the wheels that carried the truck's 1.7-ton capacity. And by the end of that year, Scania began a tradition of building its own engines.

The company grew into Scania-Vabis in 1911 following a merger with Vabis of Södertalje. But the name Scania is Latin for the southern Swedish province of Skane in whose capital, Malmö, the first factory was situated.

Today the company has a worldwide focus. Almost 95 percent of Scania trucks are sold outside the borders of Sweden. And of the 23,800 employees, a mere 10,500 are situated within the country's boundaries. Production facilities can be found in Europe and Latin America, with Scania trucks being sold in about 100 countries throughout the world.

4-SERIES, CLASS L
BUILT FOR HIGH SPEEDS AND LONG HAULS

If the L stands for anything in the naming of Scania's L Series, it's "long haul." This truck was designed specifically for high-quality highways and high speeds over long distances, typically as a tractor-semi-trailer combination or as a truck with a full trailer.

Powering the L Series are engine options ranging from a nine-liter, 310-hp unit up to the 14-liter, 530-hp V8. With the L's air intake located at the front of the cab, a few extra inches are added to the rear for longer loads.

The chassis' design allows such customization as a fifth wheel height as low as 4 inches. And the frames are available in three different strength classes—the F800 for two-axle models, the F950 for two- and three-axle models, and the F958 for three axles. Although fuel tanks may be specified individually, the two 158-gallon tanks available in aluminum or steel can ensure enough fuel for the long haul.

The truck's air suspension is available exclusively at the rear or as a full suspension. And with the latter option, the loading platform on a 4-Series truck can be tilted with the control of a hand-held unit, making it easier to handle loads. (In the case of a tractor, raising and lowering the rear axle and fifth wheel can be enough. That's why the air suspension is only standard on the rear.) The optional full air suspension also proves its worth with the ELC—an electronic level control and load handling system. On the road, it maintains a preselected level at one of two settings, depending on the type of road surface. Not only does it help with ride comfort, but it assures a gentle ride for the cargo. And with the control unit, a driver can also program the system with two load-handling heights, making it possible to load or unload in half the time. A new higher-capacity compressor enables higher cargo weights to be handled, while the ELC reduces air consumption by 85 percent during normal operation, helping improve fuel consumption.

There are no components in the air system that protrude above the frame—even on a low chassis model loaded to its maximum weight. And there is also more clearance above the rear axle crown, so it is not necessary to specify heavier, more expensive hub-reduction axles to save space. The ELC Basic maintains a predetermined load height, useful for large, volume loads where height is critical.

Scania was also one of the first truck makers in the world to offer an electronic braking system, which replaces compressed air with electronic signals, and eliminates the lag time traditional in the application of a heavy truck's brakes. And disc brakes are less likely to fade than drum-style designs.

"The use of electronics in the braking system and powertrain is inevitable," said Rolf Harju, electrical system section manager. "The traditional enemies of the electrical system are moisture, dirt, and vibration, any of which has the potential to act unseen and unheard at vulnerable locations such as plugs and sockets and other

ABOVE The long-mileage Class L design can be powered by either 310, 340, 360, 400 or 530-hp engines, with a maximum gross weight rating of 60 tonnes.

MANUFACTURER: Scania

TRUCK: 4-Series Class L

DISTINCTIVE FEATURES: An air intake at the front of the cab that offers a few extra inches to the rear for longer loads

PREMIUM SLEEPER: CR19 Topline

mechanical points. We have vastly improved the reliability of our electrical systems by eliminating as many connections as possible and improving the sealing, mounting, and mechanical integrity of those that remain."

The "superbraking" system on the R124/144LA 4 x 2—the most powerful L class—combines EBS with large, ventilated disc brakes on all axles. A hydraulic retarder and associated exhaust brake are both operated by the brake pedal. And integrated with the gearbox, the retarder is equipped with a series of intelligent functions, helping reduce worries of brake fade on downhill grades.

Adding ABS, an exhaust brake, and Scania's hydraulic retarder, this truck is ready to stop dead. And when ABS is combined with traction control, the moving drive wheels won't even spin on slick surfaces. The TC traction control system uses ABS to prevent the loss of traction. If a wheel starts to spin, the brake is momentarily applied. Engine revs are also cut to bring the wheel under control as quickly as possible. The operating lever of the parking brake has a control position, through which the driver can check whether the brake force is sufficient to hold the vehicle still once the service brakes are released. A check valve prevents the releasing of the parking brake until air pressure in the service brake reaches 4 bar.

The overall wedge shape of the truck itself is meant to reduce head-on air resistance and is more effective than sloping back the windshield.

Renowned for its safety, the L's steel cab has been tested by swinging a one-ton weight against the pillars and rear wall, while a static load of 15 tons is also applied to the roof. After that, the doors have to be open. Forward-control cabs tend to have a short crumple zone, so the structure also had to be designed to absorb kinetic energy. While a driver's-side air bag is available, pyrotechnical seat belt pretensioners provide an even higher level of safety. Safety is further enhanced with the design's high torsional stability when cornering.

Warning systems in the Scania series manage to offer different levels of safety. For drivers worried about remaining focused on the job at hand, Scania Alert transmits tones of different pitches and regular intervals through radio loudspeakers. It can be turned off when it's not wanted. The VPS (vehicle protection system), meanwhile, is a remote-controlled alarm system that monitors the doors, hatches, and cab tilting function. When activated, a siren sounds with the flashing of the hazard lights, and the starter motor and fuel injection are cut. An assault alarm will also activate the lights. Its owners can drive with a sense of security on all fronts.

ABOVE Scania remains committed to the European tradition of vertical integration, meaning it manufactures engines and drivetrain components as well as the trucks themselves.

4-SERIES, CLASS G
A Heavy-duty Truck for Heavy-duty Work

Typically used for all-round heavy-duty operations such as hauling fuel tanks, timber, and other heavy loads, the Scania Class G is built on the same modular philosophy as other 4-Series models, allowing for a flexible design. But this is the truck for high gross weights, where a sturdy chassis is crucial, and is built for train weights of up to 150 tons and for high axle weights.

The engine range spans from the nine-liter 220-hp model to the power of a 14-liter 530-hp V8. The Class G is based on F950 and F958 frames, with the choice largely determined by cargo weights and road conditions. When a rugged rear axle is needed for demanding duties, but the truck's owner doesn't want to sacrifice comfort, the rear parabolic suspension can be combined with hub reduction. And together with a hub reduction final drive, the frame height affords the truck a high

ABOVE The 4-Series Class G is designed to tackle heavy loads over short or long hauls, with a power range of 220 to 530 hp.

MANUFACTURER: Scania

TRUCK: 4-Series Class G

DISTINCTIVE FEATURES: A sturdy chassis that can handle train weights of up to 165 tons

PREMIUM SLEEPER: CR19 Topline

ABOVE For the short haul, there are a variety of daycab designs still available for heavy loads.

BELOW Available engine power ranges between 220 and 530 hp.

ground clearance and good mobility. The hub reduction helps the truck travel in soft ground, without the risk of drive wheels digging in place, or the truck becoming bogged down. Fuel tanks are available in standard aluminized steel, and high-capacity aluminum. And like its L brethren, it offers ELC.

The G is available with a wide selection of final drives and bogies among its many options. And with an R8P832 final drive and a HE bogie, a G truck can carry 30 tons. Axle suspension designs cover all options, ranging from all-steel to full-air models, with design capacities of front axles measuring between 6.7 and 9 tons, and a design capacity of 11.5, 13, or 15 tons for single axles at the rear. The bogie capacity, meanwhile, can be specified for 19, 20, 21, 24.2, 26, or 30 tons, depending on the wheel configuration.

The truck's front spring assembly is located between the two driving axles on a central axle support. That provides a single pivot point for a large range of articulation. And torque rods link the steering axle to the frame. It is, after all, built for the heavy haul.

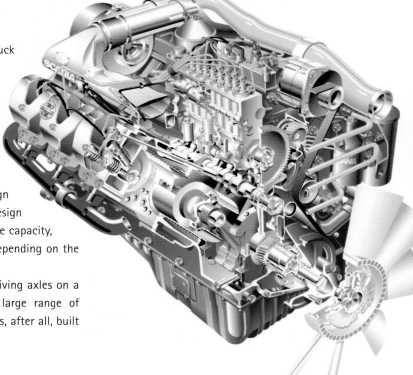

THE TOPLINE
A CAB DESIGN AT THE TOP OF THE LINE

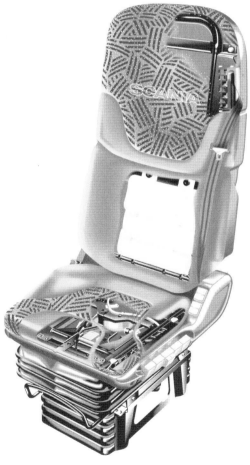

Day and sleeper versions of the L Class of trucks are available in low P and high R cabs, but the flagship cab in Scania's long-haul line is the CR19 Topline that measures 89¾ inches from floor to ceiling. Inside, the cab is 5½ inches wider than that of the 3-series. There is 31½ inches of room from the seatbacks to the rear wall of the cab when the seats are moved forward, and the overall width behind the seats measures 96½ inches.

Mounted above the windshield at the front of the cab is a 35½-inch-wide upper bed where lighting, heating, an electric roof hatch, and central locking panels are all within reach. The bed itself, which can be stowed in the roof with the help of gas springs, can be reached with a fold-down ladder.

Aircraft-style lockers offer storage space, while elasticized bands will keep clothing in place. Two storage compartments under the lower bed can be accessed from inside or outside the cab thanks to the bed's three-point construction that folds out of the way. And of course, all cabs can be equipped with such long-haul

amenities as a refrigerator, parking heater, and other accessories. Both 12- and 24-volt sockets will allow instant connections for accessories, while wiring is mounted in the standard loom for the permanent installation of most items.

The new Luxury seat saves valuable space on its own. The passenger seat can be moved out of the way against the dashboard or against the back wall, while the backrest can be folded forward to serve as a table.

Up front, the upright windshield leaves room above the driver's head for storage, and can be adapted for audio and communication devices. And throughout, ventilation is provided through 40 inlets, replacing up to 318 cubic feet of air per minute. (The sounds of the full-speed fan are muffled by mounting the unit outside of the cab.)

Comfort is further enhanced with a four-point air suspended cab, which incorporates an anti-roll bar and progressive shock absorbers.

Hinged front flaps help with daily inspections, enabling the topping up of windshield washer fluid and checks of both oil and coolant levels in only a couple of minutes. The cab's air deflectors, when properly adjusted, can reduce air resistance by up to 20 to 40 percent at 52 miles per hour, meaning a fuel saving of 10 percent. And for maintenance, they can be released from snap catches without tools. Even the steps that allow entry into the forward-control models will automatically extend and retract. Fenders attached to the chassis, meanwhile, mean no problems with dirt or spills when the cab is tilted.

THE T-CAB
A NORTH AMERICAN PROFILE IN EUROPE

For European truck owners yearning for the style of a North American design, Scania's T-Cab offers both a hood and a longer wheelbase, placing the driver behind the front axle. In the front seat, that means a smoother ride and a flat floor making it easier to move around.

Without the engine tunnel typical to COE designs, there's 68¾ inches of room from the floor to the roof. And when it's time for maintenance, the engine is easily accessed by lifting the hood by taking advantage of foot plates and grab handles.

Available as a day cab (CT 14) and as a sleeper (CT 19), the T-Cab can be specified with Scania's Class C, G, and L trucks in both tractor and rigid configurations. The ride is enhanced with a four-point air suspension, and there's added protection for the driver simply because he's placed behind the engine.

Two beds can be fitted in the sleeping section, while storage room is also accessible from outside. For that matter, the overall storage space exceeds the P and R cabs. And an optional lip-edged table can be fixed to the dashboard to brew coffee or prepare food.

While a conventional design improves aerodynamics on its own, wind resistance can be further reduced with an air deflector package. And an uncluttered rear shape enables bodywork or semi-trailers to be mounted closer to the cab. To round out the look, extra lights can be installed on the sun visor, bumper, or both.

ABOVE A bonneted design places the driver behind the front axle, for a smoother ride.

NEXT PAGE The Scania T144 LA4x2.

BELOW The design with a hood is available both as a sleeper (CT19) and as a day cab (CT14).

STERLING TRUCK CORP
WILLOUGHBY, OHIO, U.S.A.

ABOVE The premium truck in the Sterling line-up is the SilverStar, which was initially known as a Ford AeroMax.

Ford Motor Company officials boldly proclaimed a renewed focus on heavy trucks in North America with the introduction of a new product line in 1995. It was the company's first such introduction in 25 years, but Ford was back in the race. After all, it had a rich history in the trucking industry—Henry Ford built his first panel delivery truck in 1899.

But nobody saw 1997 coming. Freightliner's acquisition of the Ford heavy truck line was the surprise deal of the decade, and one of North America's biggest-ever mergers of heavy truck makers. With a deal that had its structure formed in a matter of weeks, Freightliner Corp. took control of about one third of North American heavy truck sales, and was able to round out its product offerings with a vocational truck line. The formerly Ford HN80s, which were better known as the Louisville and AeroMax, were renamed L- and A-Lines (and are built at a factory in St. Thomas, Ontario, Canada). The star attraction—an AeroMax incorporating a 77-inch sleeper— was re-born as the SilverStar.

Sterling and Freightliner have also resurrected Ford's low-cab-forward medium-duty design known as the Cargo, once a self-proclaimed World Truck and a personal favorite of Freightliner senior vice-president of engineering, Michael von Mayenburg. With a few changes such as an updated electrical system, new Cargos are returning to the road.

Already looking to expand the Sterling's reach, Freightliner will offer the trucks in Mexico by 2000 and is also selling the trucks in the traditional Ford strongholds of Australia and New Zealand.

THE A-LINE
A TRUCK BUILT AROUND DRIVERS

When Ford engineers went to work designing the A-Line, they built it around drivers—more than 900 of them. Truckers of all shapes and sizes were pulled out from behind the wheel and studied in the company's most extensive ergonomics study, which considered everything from the design of the dashboard to the placement of grab handles. And while the nameplate has changed—the truck line once known as the HN80 now carries a Sterling nameplate under Freightliner ownership—the improvements remain.

With a front axle set back 49 inches for better maneuverability and the forward transfer of weight, the A-Line is available as a 122-inch BBC long conventional (A/AT9522) and 113-inch medium conventional (A/AT9513) for those more conscious about overall length. A wheel cut of 50 degrees equally assists in tight spots. The A/AT9522 is designed for heavier work and can be powered with engines exceeding 500 hp, while a flat-top or AeroBullet bolt-on sleeper is available in addition to the SilverStar, which highlights the line-up. The A/AT9513 and its range of powertrain options can be customized for a wide range of over-the-road applications.

The A-Line's sheet-molded fiberglass doors open 55 degrees to reveal a 51 x 39-inch opening, while the seat travel ranges between 91/2 inches in the day cab to 11 inches in models incorporating a sleeper. Door windows measuring 576 square inches dip at the front, offering a better view of the road, while 9 x 12 auxiliary windows include a wide-angle Fresnel-type lens to widen the view.

But some of the most dynamic improvements are seen when the truck is moving. The rounded fairings of the A-Line boast a nine percent improvement in aerodynamics over Ford's previous L-Series, and improve fuel economy by as much as four-and-a-half percent in the process. But an optional full aerodynamics package also offers a fiberglass roof fairing with extension tabs, with other air-managing features ranging from a single roof fairing to a side extender package meant to

ABOVE A front axle set back 49 inches, with a 50-degree wheel cut, assists the driver in tight spots.

MANUFACTURER: Sterling
TRUCK: A-Line
BBC: 113, 122 inches
DISTINCTIVE FEATURES: Air intakes mounted on either side of the grille for improved engine cooling
PREMIUM SLEEPER: Aero Bullet bolt-on sleeper

LEFT The A-line dashboard was designed after an extensive study into driver ergonomics.

reduce the turbulence between cabs and trailers. Optional chassis fairings will even smooth the airflow over fuel tanks and battery boxes.

Secondary turn signals are integrated into the air-intake ports on the side of the hood, while optional, dual-faced, fender-mounted units can also be ordered. Even the optional air dam bumper with the tow hooks can remain clean; the hooks can be stored in the right frame rail when they aren't being used. The air dam, meanwhile, helps reduce the undercarriage turbulence that can harm aerodynamics.

Two openings on either side of the truck's grille—referred to as nostrils by some Sterling owners—help force a steady stream of air around the radiator, cooling under-hood temperatures by as much as five degrees Fahrenheit.

The opening of the hood itself is eased with the use of a torsion bar, while a centrally mounted hinge has been included to eliminate the twisting and stress that can lead to cracks. At the same time, the splash shield swings up and out of the way, unlike those in other truck designs that have to be removed separately to service the engine. The truck's outer panels are made of a heavy-gauge aluminum and form rigid "coach joints" that eliminate exposed rivets and save about 30 percent of the weight of a skin-over-frame assembly. And the truck's tare weight can be reduced further with a number of options made of aluminum, including the cab, front axle, fuel and air tanks, and centrifuse brake drums with aluminum hubs.

RIGHT Available rear suspensions include taperleaf, walking beam, four-spring, air-ride, and proprietary AirLiner designs (1). Air intakes on either side of the grille (4) cool the engine compartment by five degrees Fahrenheit on their own, while the hood that sits above an aerodynamic bumper (2) can be opened with the aid of a torsion bar and centrally mounted hinge (3).

The ride is softened with standard 54-inch parabolic taperleaf front springs that include shock absorbers for added help. Optional 60-inch springs are available for applications that require more deflection. Rear suspensions, meanwhile, vary to include taperleaf, walking beam, four-spring, AirLiner, and other air-ride designs. Specifically for the driver, fluid-filled rear hydromounts—which act much like mini shock absorbers—ease the ride of the cab, which can also incorporate an air suspension. The AirLiner air suspension is offered in 40,000- and 46,000-pound ratings for dual-drive applications. Its lateral track rods ensure proper axle alignment, and rolling lobe air bags maintain constant spring characteristics as they're compressed. And its ride height that drops as low as 8½ inches accommodates the tallest van trailers.

The attention to detail is apparent in a number of areas. Switches and door handles were designed for drivers wearing work gloves. The 20-inch wet-arm wipers have built-in spray nozzles supplied by a two-gallon reservoir to help clear the 1,644-square-inch windshield. Push-to-connect air brake fittings were designed to reduce air leaks by 70 percent. The A-Line also boasts 120,000-psi high-tensile bolted frame rails, which are nine percent stronger than the 110,000-psi rating typical of other trucks. And the instrument panel is easily serviced, with pop-out gauges and registers, and fasteners that are more easily accessed than those held in place with hidden clips.

Electrical enhancements also play their part to make the truck much easier to service. An in-dash fuse panel not only groups 50 branch circuits in one location, with blade-type fuses that don't require tools for replacements, but it also has 12 extra terminals for customized electrical installations that won't require splicing and taping. In many maintenance matters, it's a truck line that earns an A.

THE SILVERSTAR
THE STAR OF STERLING'S A-LINE

Sterling makes no secret that the SilverStar—the star of its A-Line—is a tractor marketed specifically to owner-operators.

It's a truck built for comfort, with a 77-inch-long sleeper and amenities ranging from a leather-wrapped steering wheel to fully adjustable seats, cruise control, tilt steering, and a premium sound system.

Available in the long conventional 122-inch BBC measurement, and as a 113-inch medium conventional, the SilverStar design offers room to stand up throughout. And the sleeper incorporates such things as a separate control panel for heating and air conditioning, radio controls, privacy curtains, and closet space that incorporates hanger rods. There is also extensive lighting.

The lower bunk offers a six-inch-thick mattress with an inner spring, while the swing-up bunk can be similarly specified, or ordered as a foam-stuffed model. To keep the elements shut out when it's time to use the beds, sleeper walls have been padded with R-6 insulation. Meanwhile, an emergency exit is available on the

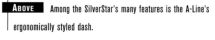

ABOVE Among the SilverStar's many features is the A-Line's ergonomically styled dash.

LEFT As the pride of the line-up, the SilverStar comes with a 77-inch-long sleeper.

MANUFACTURER: Sterling

TRUCK: SilverStar

BBC: 113, 122 inches

DISTINCTIVE FEATURES: A-Line attributes with luxury additions

PREMIUM SLEEPER: 77 inches

right hand side, along with such options as privacy shades for the upper windows, a refrigerator/freezer, a TV/VCR preparation package, a roof-mounted vista window, and a pull-out writing table. Inside, the climate is controlled with 15 separate ventilation outlets, four different blower speeds and up to eight air distribution settings, while an optional environmental filter can be designed to trap fine dust and pollen.

For those in weight-sensitive applications, aluminum options include a cab, front axle, lightweight battery boxes, fuel and air tanks, and centrifuse brake drums with aluminum hubs. Still, those who choose not to order aluminum cabs don't have to worry about rust. Other cabs are protected from corrosion by an E-coat immersion priming and epoxy sealants in a fully welded design. The hood and doors are also made of a die-formed sheet molded compound (SMC) fiberglass.

VOLVO TRUCK CORP
SWEDEN

ssar Gabrielsson and Gustav Larson weren't thinking about trucks when they sat down to lunch in 1924. They had met to discuss plans to develop a national car.

Each of the men brought distinct skills to the table. Gabrielsson was managing director of Svenska Kullagerfabriken (SKF) at the time, while Larson had studied engineering. The pair soon enlisted the help of Henry Westerberg to analyze the costs of such a venture before setting out to look for financial backers. Still, few backers could be found. Gabrielsson ultimately had to produce the money himself to open the first factory with 10 workers in 1926.

It wasn't long, though, before Volvo also began looking at trucks. Even before production began on the first car, engineers were at the drawing table, and the first truck left the plant in February 1928. Powered by four-cylinder, 28-hp gasoline engines, the design ran with three-speed transmissions and fixed wood wheels.

Final drive ratios of 6.63:1 and 7.43:1 represented the difference between two types of the early trucks, with top speeds of 31 and 24.8 miles per hour, respectively.

BELOW Volvo's truck lines were the company's most profitable venture for decades.

The wheelbase of the shorter version was 130 inches, and the longer was 145 inches. The short version, which comes without a cab and platform costs SKr 3,050 to build and sold for SKr 4,450.

The company was wise to expand their initial plans to include trucks. The first series sold out after six months, eclipsing the interest in the company's first cars. In fact, profits from making trucks financed Volvo operations for 20 years, and the company sold its car business to Ford in 1999.

Volvo in Latin means "I roll." And roll forward it has.

ABOVE If the cabover market expands in North America, Volvo Trucks could easily fit FH designs into its production lines on both sides of the Atlantic Ocean.

THE FM
BUILT WITH AN EYE TO STRENGTH

The standard Volvo Winter White color belies the rugged nature of Volvo's FM cab. Perhaps it's appropriate that there are another 50 colors from which to choose.

The Volvo FM cab is meant primarily for regional distribution and construction application, but, fitted with such cabs as the Globetrotter, it's still capable of longer distances. It's available in a range including day, sleeper, and a two-man, high-roof Globetrotter cabs, as well as standard or C-level trim options inside.

With the steel Globetrotter sleeper, the truck offers a home for two-man operations handling 18 to 20 tons through to maximum train weights.

Entry into the cab is eased with a low-level step coupled by doors that open 90 degrees. While many of the truck's features are similar to those of its predecessor, the FL, there's more living space thanks to a doghouse that sits 6¼ inches lower. Storage even includes an optional document case with a lid that functions as a worktop, while the steering wheel converts into a writing surface.

Drivers are protected from the outside world with both a four-point cab suspension and improved noise supression. And this truck line, too, features Z-cam drum brakes, with a standard exhaust brake and the option of an engine brake on the 12-liter engine. The Volvo engine brake that can be equipped to the D12 offers 320 bhp stopping power—that's the equivalent of an FM10 trying to hold the truck back. Each truck is also fitted with standard ABS.

As a way to deter theft, the trucks can be fit with an electronic starter inhibitor and antitheft alarm system as an accessory.

Inside, the sprung mattress in the sleeper cab measures 27½ x 78¾ x 5 inches, with storage including two external lockers. The Globetrotter options build on this with two bunks, an extra-high roof, and more storage. And each bunk can be equipped with a control panel that includes a clock, interior light, cabin thermostat, and power controls for the stereo. A smoke alarm is also standard. Seats are available in three levels—Comfort, Standard, and Economy—with the interior trim packages available at a Standard level or textile-based C trim. And in terms of lighting, reading lamps are fitted on a 20-inch flexible arm. Outside, lighting can be enhanced with a range of powerful spot and fog lamps made of zinc-plated steel with white or yellow lenses. The workplace lamps fitted with a built-in handle can be rotated.

For weight-conscious bulk haulers, there's the option of aluminum wheels that weigh in 33 pounds under that of their steel counterparts. And for those who work in the extreme cold that's well known in Sweden there is the Thermo 90 parking heater. The 9.2-KW two-stage heater uses outside air to improve air quality in the cab. Once the cab reaches the desired temperature, the engine is heated. (A conventional air-to-air design is more popular in the U.K.)

Volvo's load indicator system interacts with the air suspension to measure axle pressure, load weight, and gross weight for the truck and trailer. Its symbol-driven controls are fitted in the radio compartment.

MANUFACTURER: Volvo

TRUCK: FM

DISTINCTIVE FEATURES: Rugged design meant primarily for regional distribution and construction applications

PREMIUM SLEEPER: High-roof Globetrotter

LEFT The body-in-white production process used to build an FM cab (1) ensures it can easily be built as a day cab (2), with a standard sleeper (3), or a high-roof Globetrotter cab (4). For those who want added comfort, there are also C-level trim options (5).

POINTS OF IMPACT

The Swedish Impact Test

- a static load of up to 15 tons is placed on the roof, measuring twice the curb weight;
- a one-ton pendulum is swung 3 yards into the windshield pillar at an angle of 15 degrees;
- a one-ton pendulum measuring 5 feet 3 inches by 18 inches swings three yards into the rear wall of the cab.

In each case, the test is carried out on the same cab.

The EC Impact Test

- the roof is placed under a 10-ton static load;
- the front impact test is performed 4½ feet from the ground, with the pendulum hitting the cab from the front of an area of 21½ square feet;
- a 440-pound per ton payload capacity is placed from the rear.

Each test is carried out on an individual cab.

The Volvo Addition

- a half barrier impact test that simulates a typical rear-end collision.

THE FH
A TRUCK FOR GLOBETROTTERS

MANUFACTURER: Volvo

TRUCK: FH

BBC: 90.9 inches

DISTINCTIVE FEATURES: A cab design that meets the most stringent crash tests in the world

PREMIUM SLEEPER: Globetrotter XL

For Volvo, a name can say it all. What could be a better description for a long-haul truck than that of "Globetrotter?" That's the cab design that sits at the top of the FH range first introduced in 1993. The standard sleeper cab on the FH 12/16 has a BBC of 90.9 inches and a height of 87½ inches. The Globetrotter GT, meanwhile, offers a BBC stretching to 90.9 inches as well, but with a height of 103 inches. The Globetrotter XL stretches 110 inches high. Powering the trucks are engines with displacements of 12 and 16 liters, and five power ratings of between 340 and 520 hp. And the VEB engine brake offers promises to increase the normal life of service brakes by at least 25 percent. (The option fitted on 12-liter engines offers 325 braking horsepower at 2,100 rpm.) The FH is available in a variety of wheelbases, with front axle loads ranging from 5.8 to 14½ tons, axle configurations from 4 x 2 to 8 x 4, and load capacities from 10½ to 23½ tons.

Volvo, however, has made a name developing vehicles not only for their use while in service, but for protecting drivers in the event of accidents. The company first began testing cab safety in 1960, forming its own truck accident investigation team, and incorporates both the Swedish impact test and its own barrier crash test. A standard air bag highlights FH safety features, but it's coupled with a smoothed dashboard, energy absorbing materials, three-point seat belts, and netting that serves to protect passengers in the bunk.

The cage system used to develop the company's cars can also be found in the truck, with a framework of pressed sheet steel forming a protective cage around the driver. Doors are fitted with longitudinal beams that transfer energy to the rear of the cab. And antiburst locks are designed to ensure not only that the doors stay intact, but that they remain closed in the event of an accident. Then there's the added peace of mind with a standard smoke alarm.

The truck is also designed with the environment in mind, with more than 50 low-solvent water-based top coats from which to choose, and plastic trim panels that can be recycled at the end of the truck's life. In fact, more than 90 percent of the materials used to make the truck can be recycled.

Inside the cab, drivers have 82½ inches of stand-up height in front of the seats, with at least 76 inches of space above the engine tunnel. A separate writing top fits onto the steering wheel rim, and is normally stored underneath the dashboard.

The C specification range includes such additions as a heated driver's seat, added speakers for the stereo, wipers for the headlamps, full cloth trim, a passenger door that locks by remote, and tinted glass. And at the top of the range is the CD cab, which includes plush trim, enhanced dashboard, driving lamps, fog lamps, electrically controlled mirrors, and automatic air conditioning. Optional full-leather seating with electric controls can round out the look.

The cabs of FH trucks can be matched to a wide variety of demands, including areas for a mobile telephone, radio, communications radio, CD player, and loudspeakers. Standard features in the sleeper cab include an air-suspended driver's seat with lumbar control, a night heater, cruise control, and a radio cassette player

that sits in the dash. And for longer distances, there are additional options available in the Globetrotter and Globetrotter XL cabs.

The standard glass roof hatch makes the interior even lighter. And not only is it electrically operated, but it's provided with a perforated shutter that functions both as an insect net and sun visor.

Three large shelving compartments that are fitted with doors are found high up on the cab rear wall, and are supplemented by a large surface top on which to place items above the radio shelf. Three compartments below the lower spring-filled bunk include a lockable pull-out drawer and two compartments that can be accessed from outside the truck. One compartment can be opened from the inside and can be used to install a refrigerator box. A compartment for storing small items, meanwhile, is stored next to the gearshift lever and functions as a footstep up to the top bunk.

A control panel at the rear wall also helps control the lights, radio, and heater. Above the driver area, there's even the opportunity to install a TV or microwave shelf.

A standard chassis height on two-axle versions of the truck is ideal for typical fifth wheel heights of 51 inches with 80-series tires. And the 35½-inch version requires a 43.3-inch fifth-wheel height on 70-series tires when more load volume is needed in those European runs that allow a maximum height of 13 feet. A FH12 low-height tractor offers a 37-inch fifth wheel height in conjunction with low-profile 295/60R 22.5 tires. In turn, the latter tractor features a lighter frame and S parabolic rear springs to improve the ride and axle locations. Those springs are not only road-friendly in the eyes of the European Union, but will still be worthy of heavier weights if the U.K. increases the weights of its trains.

TOP AND ABOVE Volvo's commitment to safety can be seen everywhere from extensive crash tests (top) to the restraints used to protect sleeping co-drivers (bottom).

A 23-ton design rear air suspension is available for a road-friendly ride. And on the heavy end, an FH12/16 T-ride offers a 28½-ton multi-leaf suspension and hub reduction axles for heavy hauls of up to 165 tons.

All FH models feature a synchromesh gearbox that's matched to the specific engine. With an FH12 340 and 380, there's a simple eight-speed range change unit, or the 12-speed range change and splitter box. Both units feature a crawler gear. For heavier hauls and higher power, the FH12 420 and FH16 feature a six-speed range box with a splitter on each gear for 12 forward gears and two crawlers. Except for the FH16 520 model, each gearbox features a direct top gear ratio to reduce losses due to friction in the drivetrain. The FH12 models have the option of a Volvo Geartronic automatic mechanical gearbox based on a 12-speed splitter design, with hold and performance buttons, which are there to help operate the truck on hills and traffic circles.

All of the on-road trucks are fitted with single-reduction rear axles. (Hub reduction versions are available for heavy hauls.) Differential locks are standard, with double drive models featuring axle locks and interaxle cross locks.

Volvo's Z-cam drum brake, meanwhile, is meant to spread the braking force across the shoe, with an internal self adjuster. Large lining areas, a two-stage exhaust brake on 16-liter engines, and the Volvo engine brake on 12-liter models offer increased brake life.

VOLVO TRUCKS NORTH AMERICA
GREENSBORO, NORTH CAROLINA

Perhaps there's little surprise that Volvo Trucks would come to North America. When Assar Gabrielsson and Gustav Larson built their first commercial trucks in 1928, the Swedish truck makers incorporated many American concepts, including a four-cylinder, 28-hp gasoline engine and a three-speed transmission with fixed wooden wheels. In some respects, the trucks even looked like the Pierce-Arrow, with its bug-eyed headlamps.

Volvo Trucks moved into North America in 1981, when the company purchased the White Motor Corporation and transformed it into the Volvo White Truck Corporation. A joint venture with General Motors Corporation followed in 1987, leading to the Volvo-GM Heavy Truck Corporation and the WhiteGMC nameplate.

In 1995, though, the company created a nameplate of its own. Volvo is now the only identity given to today's trucks. In 1997, the company became Volvo Trucks North America. With its line of diesel engines, transmissions, and rear suspensions, the Greensboro, North Carolina, truck maker is one of the few North American truck manufacturers that make proprietary components.

BELOW Unveiled in 1996, the VN Series was heralded as the safest cab Volvo Trucks North America had ever built.

THE VN SERIES
SAFETY FIRST

Volvo engineers must grin at the thought that they crushed 13 VN Series cabs before the first truck was even sold. It was a question of safety first, and the answers were in the crash tests.

The VN Series unveiled in 1996 was heralded as the safest cab Volvo Trucks North America had ever built, proven by an extensive shopping list of safety features. It was one of the first trucks on the continent to offer an optional air bag (now a standard); there is a collapsible steering column and deformable steering wheel; and Kevlar-enforced knee bolsters are designed to absorb the impact of a driver's knees if they slide forward in an accident. With an absence of North American crash standards, this cab even meets the demands of the Swedish Impact Test—the standard upon which the European ECE R-29 crash-worthiness criteria are based.

The cab is Volvo's strongest ever, with high strength steel (HSS) construction designed for a million-mile life. (The same material is used to build the Volvo 850 passenger car.) Still, the look of the truck isn't a radical departure from previous Volvo designs—barring aerodynamically sculpted fenders and a passenger-side-mounted grille that acts as an air intake for the engine—but there is a wide range of improvements.

MANUFACTURER: Volvo Trucks North America

TRUCK: The VN Series

BBC: 113, 123 inches

DISTINCTIVE FEATURES: A crashworthy cab design with an array of safety features including an air bag

PREMIUM SLEEPER: 770

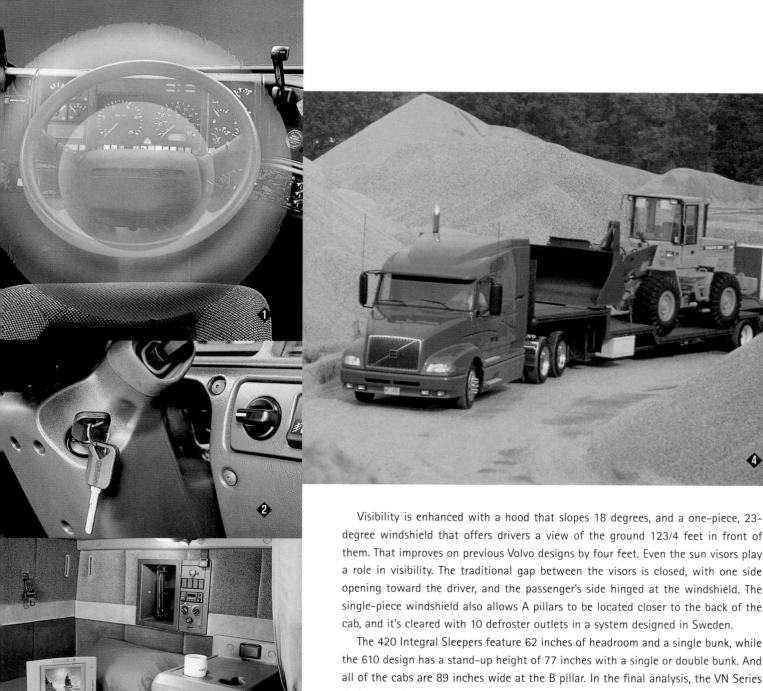

ABOVE In 1999, Volvo became the first truck maker in North America to offer standard driver's side air bags (1), but that isn't the VN Series' only unique feature. An on-column starter (2) helps set this truck apart as does a well-designed work station (3). Although it can work in demanding environments (4), a well-insulated design ensures that the interior remains quiet.

Visibility is enhanced with a hood that slopes 18 degrees, and a one-piece, 23-degree windshield that offers drivers a view of the ground 123/4 feet in front of them. That improves on previous Volvo designs by four feet. Even the sun visors play a role in visibility. The traditional gap between the visors is closed, with one side opening toward the driver, and the passenger's side hinged at the windshield. The single-piece windshield also allows A pillars to be located closer to the back of the cab, and it's cleared with 10 defroster outlets in a system designed in Sweden.

The 420 Integral Sleepers feature 62 inches of headroom and a single bunk, while the 610 design has a stand-up height of 77 inches with a single or double bunk. And all of the cabs are 89 inches wide at the B pillar. In the final analysis, the VN Series designs are four inches taller, five inches deeper, and six inches wider than were the previous models.

In the cab's header, glove-compartment-like doors hold items in storage bins, while a cup holder slides out of the halfway point in the dash. Another cup holder is available at the base of the dash, which includes an inset spot to offer room for the handle of a mug.

In an effort to keep out noise and the elements, each door incorporates two seals, and a shifter boot covers the entire stick from below the floor, which itself incorporates an inch of insulation. In addition to the added insulation, an independently mounted exhaust helps muffle the sounds of the ride. When the elements do close in, rain is diverted onto the roof with deflectors on each side of the windshield, rubber fins at the bottom of mirror housings pull water down and away, and channeled inner fenders and splash shields are used to lessen splash and spray. Controls on the stalk of the steering column include a single-touch feature that calls for a single swipe of the wipers to clear the windshield.

The VN Series is available as a 113-inch medium conventional and 123-inch conventional in single- or tandem-axle configurations.

THE 770
BUILT FOR COMFORT

MANUFACTURER: Volvo Trucks North America

TRUCK: 770

BBC: 123 inches

DISTINCTIVE FEATURES: Volvo's largest integrated sleeper design, measuring 77 inches from the back of the driver's seat to the back wall

When it was time for Volvo's VN Series to grow up, it did so in a big way. The Volvo 770 Integral Sleeper was unveiled with 566 cubic feet of room, measuring 77 inches from the back of the driver's seat to the back wall. Although it's built on the chassis of the VN Series, this truck is new from the chassis upward, and is presented as the flagship of Volvo Trucks North America.

Amenities ranging from a refrigerator and microwave to an entertainment system and dinette are among a wide range of comforts often sought by drivers for what has to become a home away from home.

And they're all here. The top bunk of the sleeper comes complete with a ladder to help those who have to climb a little higher to sleep on a 39 x 79-inch sprung mattress. Below, another spring-softened mattress measures 42 x 79 inches.

In terms of storage, the 770 has 78 cubic feet of space on shelves and under the bunk, while clothes can hang side to side thanks to the added closet space. Floor-to-ceiling cabinets are found behind the driver's and passenger's seats, and there are also two levels of side-to-side storage above the windshield, under-bunk storage

with in-cab access and outside luggage compartment access, a footwell storage area in the sleeper, and upper and lower storage units on the back wall.

Optional leather seats for the driver can even be heated in a feature also found in Volvo car interiors, while a new air-ride cab suspension helps smooth the ride.

When it's time to set down a drink, there are 10 cup holders available—two in the central work table, two for the upper bunk, two for the lower bunk, a dual cup holder in the engine tunnel, and a dual cup holder in the dash. Ashtrays are built in the bunk's master control panel and the dash, while there are five 12-volt outlets and two cigar lighters. The power supply is further enhanced with a 110-volt power source for an optional computer workstation.

Air supplies are cleaned with separate filters found in both the cab and the sleeper. And when it's time to relax, there's a 200-watt sound system, television and VCR, including a CD player and remote control, and an omnidirectional TV antenna. Other options include nine speakers to enhance the sound, including the sub-woofer for the sleeper area.

ABOVE With the bunks folded out of the way, there's plenty of room to move around a central work table.

NEXT PAGE The raised roof design helps reduce aerodynamic drag.

WESTERN STAR TRUCKS
CANADA

As one of the youngest truck makers in the world, Western Star Trucks, based in Kelowna, British Columbia, Canada, has experienced its fair share of growing pains. The now-defunct White Motor Co. built the Western Star plant in 1967, taking advantage of a government initiative to diversify the region's agriculture-dependent economy. And it found some success. Although Western Star was first devoted to Class 8 trucks for logging, mining, and oil exploration (a Class 8 truck has a GVW of more than 33,000 pounds), it expanded in the next decade to build highway trucks for owner-operators.

But the troubles began in 1981. When White went bankrupt, Volvo purchased its American assets and left the Canadian business behind. The Kelowna operation was bought by Canadian-based investors from Nova Corporation and Bovar Investments. The investment, however, wasn't enough on its own. The new owners were faced with the daunting task of rebuilding a dealer network in the United States. At the same time, the North American economy was plunging into a recession; the trucking industry itself was fighting through the early years of deregulation in the U.S., with Canada soon to follow.

As the battles were fought, the debt load began to mount, and those assembling the trucks at a successful Western Star operation in Australia saw their source of components at risk. They began to seek a new source of money. Help came in 1991 when Western Star International Pte—a Singapore company associated with the Peabody family—took control of the truck maker. Offices in Nashville, Tennessee, and Toronto, Canada, were pulled back to the home base of Kelowna. Operating costs were slashed by 40 percent and the company launched a renewed focus on traditional Western Star buyers found in owner-operators and small fleets.

With a Canadian military contract to build Light Support Vehicle Wheeled (LSVW) trucks in 1992, the business began to find its feet again. The Kelowna plant was expanded in 1994 to 260,000 square feet. And the company's first all-new truck design since 1967—the Constellation Series—was unveiled in 1996. The business also expanded, with an acquisition of Orion Bus Industries in 1995, and the purchase of U.K.-based ERF in 1996 to give the company access to European and African markets. In 1999, it announced plans to build a U.S. manufacturing facility.

THE CONSTELLATION SERIES
A STAR ATTRACTION FROM CANADA

Perhaps the Rocky Mountains of Canada is an appropriate birthplace for Western Star's rugged Constellation Series. Launched in 1996, the redesigned cab ended a four-decade-long engineering drought for the manufacturer. Six new models—the 4800FX, 4900EX, 4900 FX, 4900SX, 5800SX, and 5900SS—were built on the visibility of the company's previous line, but still stayed true to the long-nose conventional look that remains its selling point.

And to Western Star, bigger is better. Sleeper sizes include a 45-inch, 58-inch low roof, 58-inch high roof, and 72-inch model, all of which have two separate exterior access storage compartments. A 34-inch sleeper is targeted at specialized vocational applications, traditionally a strongpoint of the Western Star strategy.

Size, however, isn't always associated with weight. Initially criticized for its weight, the Constellation Series has steadily shaved pounds from its cab since its introduction. For example, by replacing steel siding with a polypropylene honeycomb sandwiched between two skins of aluminum, the 76-inch SLS (Star Light Sleeper) tips the scales at 15,840 pounds, saving 400 pounds when compared to initial Constellation Series designs. About 200 pounds were shaved from 45-inch models. Eight of the 12 panels used to build the sleeper can incorporate the sandwich-like designs, bonded together using a combination of urethane adhesive and mechanical fasteners. Doors and other areas of the cab are expected to see the technology, too. Comfort is enhanced with two air bags mounted at the mid-point of the sleeper and the outboard of the frame rails.

ABOVE Western Star remained true to its long-nosed styles with the redesigned Constellation Series.

MANUFACTURER: Western Star

TRUCK: Constellation Series

DISTINCTIVE FEATURES: A lightweight option built with honeycomb-filled panels

PREMIUM SLEEPER: 76-inch Star Light Sleeper

For resale value, the ability to shed a sleeper to create a day cab for a future user is crucial. "And as far as we know, it's the easiest to convert in the industry," boasted Glen Ashdown, the chief engineer behind the project.

Sometimes, it's the first impression that's responsible for attracting buyers. So the Constellation Series cleaned up the look of previous designs in several ways, with such improvements as wiring routed through the arms of a five-arm, forward-mounting West Coast mirror. Even the entry is easier than ever. The Constellation doors are four inches wider and 2¾ inches higher than previous designs, while there's 3½ inches more headroom, two inches more knee room, and belly room that expands by two to four inches.

On the dash, an Electronic Control Center not only incorporates information from engine control modules, but also handles windshield wiper/washer controls, dash light dimming, daytime running lights, and the signal light flasher, as well as controlling the fan and shutting down the engine.

Bezels surrounding gauges aren't only available in a standard black, but are available with an optional 23-karat gold plating for the more luxury-minded owner-operator. Rocker switches have illuminated symbols for better visibility, while gauge numbers are also lit from behind.

In the overhead console, lights are available through an optional reading-light package and adjustable lights above the doors. A dome light is located at the center of the cab, while an optional courtesy-light package is also available in the lower portion of the doors.

Outside, dual rectangular headlamps are adjustable from the front of the hood, while aero hoods use side intakes to reduce premature clogging. The assembly itself is attached to the hood with self-locking nuts and is available in stationary or hood-mounted versions. For colder nights, the Constellation Series' new climate control package improves on Western Star's previous heating capacity by 60 percent, and cooling is bettered by 97 percent. The defrosting system has dedicated side window outlets in the top of the door trim panel for improved visibility. And in tests that were conducted in Thunder Bay, Ontario, Canada, windows became clear in as little as 10 minutes.

The new air system offers standard washable, replaceable dust filters, and optional filters to handle dust and odors. With these and other amenities, Constellation Series owners can simply breathe easy.

A HIGHER POWER

THE MOST POWERFUL TRUCK
ENGINES IN THE WORLD

CATERPILLAR: THE 3406E

THE KING OF THE HILL

Caterpillar set a horsepower benchmark for the world with its 550-hp 3406E engine, proclaiming it to be nothing less than the "King of the Hill." However in 1997, the 3406E became the first engine to break that barrier, with a power range extended to 600 hp. The 15.8-liter 3406E offers 2,050 lb-ft of torque at 2,100 rpm while still using much of the componentry of its 14.6-liter cousin.

The power wasn't simply created by boring out the 550-hp design either. A new camshaft has a changed lobe profile, there's a higher peak cylinder pressure on the cylinder block, and a 3.2-mm longer stroke on the crank. The Electronic Unit Injector (EUI) runs at 30,000 KSI PIP, the liner has a 2.5-mm larger bore, and the new piston crown, skirt, and rings can boast a 2.5-mm larger bore.

In a test drive from Chicago to San Francisco, when compared to its 550-hp predecessor at 1,850 lb-ft torque, the newer engine required 40 shifts instead of 140. With a Jacobs 340A engine retarder operating at 1,700 rpm on an 80,000 GCW rig, speeds hold at 31 miles per hour on a six percent grade, 42 miles per hour on a five percent grade, and 57 miles per hour on a four percent grade without other brakes being applied.

The cylinder block has a deep-skirt, cast iron alloy design made of 30,000-psi minimum strength cast iron. The one-piece cylinder head incorporates the air manifold in the same casting, meaning fewer gaskets, bolts, and washers. And the crankshaft is hardened in Caterpillar furnaces.

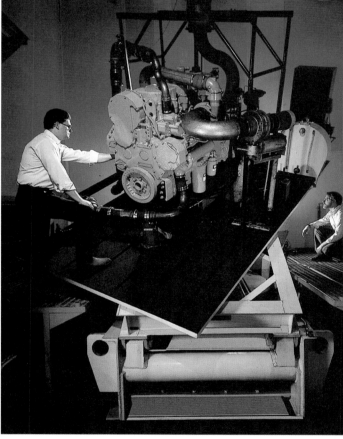

Fuel is delivered with mechanically actuated, electronically controlled unit injectors, as well as state-of-the-art electronic controls. And injectors are housed in stainless-steel sleeves, isolating them from combustion gases and engine coolant. The turbocharger includes a boreless compressor wheel that reduces the possibility of low-cycle fatigue, while peak cylinder pressure is limited with the wastegate turbocharger that also lowers heat rejection and the turbocharger's speed. The overhead camshaft and drivetrain is meant to ensure precise valve timing, while the valve train eliminates the need for valve bridge adjustments because there are no valve lifters, push rods/tubes, or bridge dowels.

The engine monitoring system keeps an eye on such things as oil pressure, and the temperature and level of the coolant, and can be programmed to provide different levels of protection. The brain of the operation—the Electronic Control Module—tracks information and relays feedback on diagnostics, mileage, and fueling. That information can then be fed to drivers through the Cat Driver Information Display (Cat ID), which also offers a theft deterrent feature that can require a password before the engine will start.

ABOVE Caterpillar engineers observe a 3406E on a tilt table—one of the many tests designed to determine engine performance under severe operating conditions.

Engine data can even be sent to a remote location with a system that marries OmniTRACS and Highway Master communications systems. With this, a home office can access non-operating parameters including the distance the truck has traveled, how much fuel has been consumed, and engine hour intervals, as well as fault alerts related to specific problems.

CUMMINS: THE SIGNATURE SERIES
RED, HOT, AND HIGH HORSES

The Signature Series features 600 hp and 2,050 lb-ft torque and dual overhead cams, an integrated engine brake delivering 600 hp of braking force, and a 50,000-mile oil drain interval. With a high-pressure electronically controlled fuel system, the 15-liter power unit has a bore and stroke of 137 x 169 mm, with a dry weight of 2,610 pounds. And by integrating the new Cummins Intebrake built by Jacobs, the 600 hp of retarding power is added with a weight of no more than 20 pounds.

The smallest of two cams has lobes designed specifically for braking, so the Intebrake doesn't need to be activated by an injector lobe or exhaust lobe in the approach typical to single-camshaft designs. There are six brake settings plus automatic cruise control. The first, larger injector cam delivers fuel with 28,000 psi of pressure, while the open-nozzle design is meant to cut noise and emissions.

Heavy-duty rings, pistons, and bearings, meanwhile, are all designed to last. A smaller injector package is created by moving four solenoids to the fuel system module, bolted to the side of the head adjacent to the fuel injection cam.

The Signature Series' variable output turbocharger is meant to work like a small turbo at low speeds, but act like a big turbo at high speeds, when a low back pressure is needed. The air compressor, meanwhile, only turns on when a Signature-equipped truck is traveling downhill. The Electronic Control Module for this engine has been integrated into the cylinder head, with a Gore-Tex-covered vent allowing it to breathe. The component itself is cooled by a hole in the cylinder head. The fuel pump, fuel filter, and electronics can all be found under a single panel.

ABOVE Advancements in the Signature Series' electronic control module allow changes to be programmed with the use of short-range radio frequencies. No plugs are required.

DETROIT DIESEL: THE SERIES 60
A LEADER IN ELECTRONIC ENGINES

ABOVE Detroit Diesel was the first engine maker in North America to control fuel injection electronically.

At the upper end of Detroit Diesel's Series 60, is a 500-hp model rated at 2,100 rpm and offering 1,650 lb-ft of torque at 1,200 rpm. The Series 60's overhead camshaft design eliminates push rods, lifters, and 40 wear surfaces, and a channel machined in the top of the liner and the block allows engine coolant to flow around the liner, offering cooler cylinder temperatures and a longer life for rings and pistons.

With the two-piece cast iron crosshead piston and the plateau-honed cast iron cylinder liner, small clearances are possible. The resulting design offers stronger parts, less wear during a cold start-up, reduced noise, and lower exhaust emissions. Additional strength can be found throughout the engine. By fastening eight headbolts per cylinder, for example, the clamping load is more uniform, and one million pounds of clamping force holds the head to the block to eliminate the fear of head gasket leaks. The Detroit Diesel Electronic Controls (DDEC) has, among other functions, a feature allowing four horsepower ratings to be stored in the engine and changed when it's time to sell the truck for another application. The DDEC III electronic controls include an Electronically Erasable Programmable Read Only Memory Chip (EEPROM) with the operating software that controls horsepower, torque, and maximum engine speed. Because electronics control injection timing and the quantity of fuel, the Series 60 can start unaided at temperatures as low at 10.4° Fahrenheit.

IVECO: THE MIGHTY V-8
HIGH POWER AT LOW REVS

Capable of delivering 514 hp at 1,900 rpm, the 520-hp IVECO V8 engine offers 2,200 Nm of torque at only 1,100 rpm. That's the top of the line for EuroStar engines that range from 420 hp. The 17.2-liter turbo intercooled engine incorporates a new piston design, improved seven-hole injection, revised cylinder head design, new combustion chamber shape, and a viscostatic fan control system for better fuel economy and lower emissions. Plug-in MODUS diagnostics interact with the engine, air suspension, and brake systems. Its three sensors—two on the flywheel and one on the fuel injection pump—provide torque readings for each cylinder.

Drain intervals, meanwhile, have been stretched to 31,000 miles. And for easier daily servicing, the oil dipstick and filler cap, radiator header, clutch fluid reservoir, and screen washer tank are all grouped together.

EuroTech electronics feature a 55-amp alternator and starter motors from 4.0 to 6.6k W. And the engines themselves are fitted standard with the Semi-Automated Mechanical Transmission (SAMT), making it easier for drivers to stay in the "double green zone" where the best fuel economy is found. With it, three electro-pneumatic cylinders do the shifting, leaving the clutch to be used for only starting and stopping.

ABOVE IVECO has built a name for itself as one of the world's leading builders of commercial vehicle diesel engines.

MACK TRUCKS: THE E-TECH
BUILDING ON THE E7 V-MAC

Mack Trucks built on its 12-liter E7 E-Tech engine with the Vehicle Management and Control System, known as V-MAC III. With three families and 10 power ratings ranging from 275 to 460 hp, the resulting E-Tech offers the added benefit of retarding power through its J-Tech engine brake. The engine's electronic unit pump fuel system operates at 26,000 psi, compared to the 18,000 psi of the E7, better atomizing the fuel and improving both combustion and fuel economy. (Inlet ports and piston bowl design create a swirling motion in the cylinder, offering up to 10 times the rotational energy of competing systems.)

Coupled with the V-MAC III's fuel and timing controls, the engine's throttle response is 30 percent quicker than the previous generation E7 engine, and there are also other electronic improvements. The low idle can be adjusted between 500 and 750 rpm, while the high idle—the maximum no-load governed speed—can be set to suit individual driving preferences.

The proprietary J-Tech engine brake offers up to 360 retarding horsepower at 2,100 rpm. And in cruise control, the brake's activation can be delayed until two miles per hour above the set speed to prevent unnecessary brake cycling, while the J-Tech disengages at a half mile per hour above the set speed.

Each cylinder has its own electronic unit pump, located on the side of the valve instead of under the valve cover. And all six pumps are driven off the third lobe of the camshaft. Each single-plunger, electronically controlled fuel pump delivers a high-pressure burst of fuel through 17-inch injection lines. Fuel injectors can also be replaced independently of the entire pumping unit.

Meanwhile, the engine retains its two-cylinder head design and a block-mounted camshaft for better stability and stress tolerances. And that overhead valve arrangement is easier to repair than other, more crowded designs.

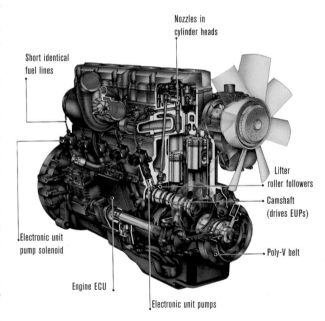

ABOVE To help in repairs, replacement pumps, injectors and fuel lines all carry the same respective part numbers for all cylinders.

MAN: THE V10 F2000
A HIGHER POWER FOR THE EUROPEAN MARKET

The Euro-2, V10-powered F2000 was unveiled in 1996, offering 603 bhp at 1,700 to 1,900 rpm, with a maximum torque of 1,991 lb-ft at 1,100 to 1,450 rpm, and a 22 percent torque rise. The V-type four-stroke diesel engine with two turbochargers, air-to-air intercooler, and wastegate offers power through ten 90-degree cylinders. Pistons displace 1,115 cubic inches, and the power plant has a compression ratio of 17:1. All power is offered in a dry weight of 2,678.6 pounds, and the power-to-weight ratio is 6 pounds/kW.

Initially, the engine was only available in four- and six-wheeled tractor units, long-wheelbase rigids used for flatbeds or intermodal bodies, all-wheel-drive six wheelers used in construction, and—of course—heavy haulage tractors. High horsepower isn't simply meant for better acceleration; there's a chance to travel at consistently higher speeds over hills, with fewer gear changes. The air intake system features compact turbine units and rapid run-up turbines with wastegates that increase torque levels at lower revolutions. If the charge turbine pressure exceeds the allowable level, the wastegate opens to stop boost pressure from rising. This engine relies on a gear-driven in-line injection pump that, in conjunction with M5 EDC, calculates the amount of fuel to be delivered. But an electronic driveline governor reduces the quantity of injected fuel preventing the engine from accelerating too quickly while preventing driveline abuse and premature tire wear. When the truck is fully laden, the pistons stroke at a rate of 9.0 m/s at the rated engine speed, with an average pressure of 18.6 bar. The maximum cut-off speed has been set at 2,150 rpm. For higher torques, the driveline includes an axle ratio of 3.36:1, combined with an overdrive top gear ratio of 0.84:1 for the 16-speed gearbox.

MERCEDES-BENZ: THE V8 500 SERIES
16 LITERS OF "GO ANYWHERE" POWER

With limited speed limits, torque is as important as horsepower, and this engine in ratings of 476, 530, and 571 hp, offers 1,992 lb-ft (2,700 Nm) of it at the top of the line. With a dry weight of 2,370 pounds, the V8 OM 502 LA also has a power-to-swept-volume ratio of up to 26.2 kW/liter of displacement, and a power-to-weight ratio of up to 2.6 kg/kW. The new "Big Cylinder" modular design is built around a core design with two liters per cylinder. Its exhaust gas turbocharging and intercooling incorporates a low-swirl combustion process, while the pump-line-nozzle high-pressure injection system offers injection pressures of up to 1,800 bar. Eight-hole injection nozzles are fitted vertically in the center of the engine head, providing room for the decompression valve of the enhanced engine brake. The engine is rated at 1,800 rpm; maximum torque is available at engine speeds as low as 1,080 rpm.

The V8 has a bore and stroke of 130 x 150 mm, with a swept volume of two liters per cylinder. With a 2,480-pound dry weight, it still produces maximum torque ratings of 2,300, 2,400, and 2,700 Nm. Its features include the Telligent electronic engine management system that offers an extensive array of diagnostics. Oil and fuel filters are found at the front of the engine, while engine oil is extracted through a tube attached to the oil sump and filter. Service intervals are stretched to 62,100 miles.

SCANIA: THE 14-LITER
HEAVY MUSCLE FOR HEAVY DEMANDS

At the top of the Scania scale is an up-rated V8 engine offering 530 hp packed into a compact design. Injection functions are separated in the cold area within the V, and the exhaust systems located outside the two banks of cylinders provide a more stable environment for a consistent mixture of air and fuel. Meanwhile, modified timing gears drive the key functions of the camshaft, injection pump, oil pump, power steering, and brake air compressor.

The turbocharger is mounted at the center, to offer higher air pressure to drive the turbine. And by increasing the air supply at the intake of the compressor, the turbo can boost acceleration at slower speeds.

The engine's eight cylinder heads are protected from high temperatures and pressures of combustion with precise clamping. The skirts of the pistons are made from aluminum, but steel crowns help withstand potential pressures of more than 23 tons. The crown's design optimizes the swirling of fuel in the combustion chamber. The ring set, meanwhile, has a high-mounted keystone compression ring near the top of the piston, minimizing the dissipation of air between piston and cylinder liner.

Belts and pulleys incorporate a multiform V-profile that leads to less lost power and maximum efficiency for alternator and water pump. An elasticized coupling links the cooling fan to the crankshaft, offering better cooling with fewer parts, while the coupling also dampens vibrations. Sensors are used to monitor an array of systems, and that data is read 20 to 100 times per second, leading to a regulated mixture of air and fuel. The circulating oil that lubricates the entire process is filtered with a two-part system that includes a centrifugal filter and renewable full-flow paper filter to grab larger particles.

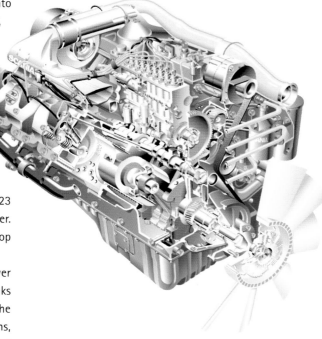

ABOVE Although it's a V8 engine, the 14-liter Scania engine is built in a more compact design than many V6 powerplants.

VOLVO: THE D16A-520
THE 16-LITER SOLUTION FOR A HIGHER POWER

With its 16-liter displacement, the Volvo D16A-520 delivers power with a maximum of 520 hp and 2,400 Nm of torque at 1,800 rpm. The in-line, six-cylinder direct injection diesel engine with turbocharger and intercooler incorporates four valves for each cylinder to allow a rapid exchange of gases, electronically controlled vertical injectors, and a camshaft mounted high on the engine. With short push rods and roller tappets also placed high, the camshaft location is better equipped to control the timing of the engine's valves. The engine runs most efficiently in its "economy" band, while drivers can access more than 90 percent of the available torque within 1.5 seconds. An exhaust brake kicks in as the accelerator pedal is released, with a maximum braking force of 275 kW. (Drivers maintain optimum engine speed with the help of an orange band on the tachometer. Meanwhile, the engine's compression ratio of 17.5:1 offers a rapid start to combustion.) The D16A-520 has an individual cylinder head for each cylinder and flame barrier. Double-lubricating oil filters and by-pass filters are coupled to an oil cooler with a thermostat-controlled flow of oil. If the engine doesn't start in cold weather more fuel is delivered through the injectors.

A gear-driven coolant pump and two sleeve thermostats improve the engine's reliability, while a by-pass filter purifies small amounts of coolant and adds rust inhibitors. An electronic control fitted within an aluminum housing is mounted behind the passenger seat, and from there outlets communicate with other systems.

ABOVE More than 90 percent of the torque available from Volvo's 16-liter engine can be reached within 1.5 seconds.

REMARKABLE TRUCKS

PUSHING THE LIMITS

It's easy to see the attraction to heavy trucks that dominate the highways of the world, with their sheer size and their gleaming of chrome. But some trucks manage to attract a different type of attention. In many cases, they're only prototypes, offering a glimpse of what may come. How comfortable can a driver be? What types of fuel will he use?

Still other trucks aren't meant for the open road at all, but simply push the limits of traditional designs. The following pages are devoted to just a few of these.

CADJEBUT'S WORKHORSE
THE WORLD'S LONGEST ROAD TRAIN

In the Kimberly region of Australia, 164-foot road trains don't deserve a second look. But in the land of long rigs, the one pulling its weight across the Cadjebut lead and zinc mine will still turn heads. The 210-ton loaded monstrosity measures 229.65 feet long, pulled by a Western Star prime mover with a 19-liter, 600-bhp engine under the hood. Even fully loaded, it can cruise at 50 miles per hour.

The 22 axles under four trailers have a tare weight of 63 tons. And they need everything a 19-liter, straight-six turbocharged Cummins KTA engine can dish out. The 18-speed Eaton transmission is linked to Rockwell differentials, while a heavy-duty six-rod mechanical suspension does what it can to control the ride. Trailers draw on the stability of leaf springs. Typical to other Outback trucks, though, it's also fitted with a heavy-duty bull bar and six-stud, fast-change wheels. Tinted windows keep out the desert sun, while twin air intake stacks are placed over the windshield to keep out the dust associated with a mining operation. The sun visor is peaked, and the top of the hood is painted black to cut down on glare further. A mesh stoneguard protects the two-piece windshield. The all-important air conditioner sits on top of the roof.

ABOVE Weighing more than 231 tons, the road train serving the Cadjebut lead and zinc mine has a top speed of 50 miles per hour.

It's a rough duty cycle—perhaps one of the roughest in the world—but the oil is changed every 250 hours, while gearbox and differential oils are changed every 1,000 hours.

The steer and trailer axles are all fitted with super single tires, although the dollies that only have a tandem wheel package incorporate dual designs to ensure a longer life. Drawbars are all 143/4 feet long to spread the impact of the load, compared to 111/2-foot lengths used by those on roads. And the tires themselves will last for about 25,000 miles.

Its fuel economy, however, will never be the envy of linehaul rigs. This combination burns 185 gallons of fuel per day.

ENVIRONMENTAL CONCEPT TRUCK
THE TRUCK WITH DESIGNS ON THE FUTURE

Volvo's Environmental Concept Truck was the result of 18 months of brainstorming, with the company's top engineers and designers bringing together all of the technology they foresee for the pick-up and delivery market. The fruits of their labor were unveiled in Sweden in 1995 as a 49-foot-long, bus-like design with a final price tag of $18 million. Too pricey for today's market? For sure. But these are simply elements to come in the world of localized trucking. And for that matter, many of the concepts could also find their way into long-haul vehicles.

The mere existence of the ECT makes it easy to see that Volvo expects environmental issues to shape future truck designs. The truck itself is powered with a hybrid driveline that blends a gas turbine with an integrated high-speed generator, batteries, and an electric motor. The final result: a truck that's electrically powered in the city and burns ethanol or another alternative fuel when traveling longer distances. Diesel be gone.

In its hybrid mode, the driveline can virtually recharge the truck's nickel-metal-hydride batteries in only 20 minutes (the time it takes to build the batteries from 20 to 80 percent). But for now, the gas turbine isn't commercially available because it consumes too much fuel, although it could be on the streets around 2010, according to Volvo officials. As for the batteries, they weigh in at a massive 4,500 pounds, so their time hasn't come just yet.

The concept vehicle doesn't limit advancements to changes in fuel supplies. With four-wheeled steering, for example, the ECT virtually moves sideways. And at low speeds, the rear wheels swivel in the opposite direction to the front wheels, cutting the vehicle's turning circle to about 56 feet. A standard truck of the same size would normally need another 10 feet to turn. At 19 miles per hour, the rear wheels begin to steer in the same direction as the front.

Where power steering usually offers the same help at every speed, the ECT's steering is enhanced with a speed-dependent design that offers lighter steering at lower speeds. And an active suspension system maintains the truck at one level over changing road surfaces, with a computer-controlled hydraulic cylinder counteracting bumps and vibrations.

There's something else missing from this truck: mirrors. Instead, video cameras monitor an area around the truck, transmitting their images to video monitors in the cab's header. Blindspots are further eliminated with a collision warning system that's activated as the truck moves into reverse.

Many of the controls normally found on the dash, meanwhile, have been moved to instrument pods attached to the steering wheel. With that, a driver's size doesn't matter. Common controls are always within easy reach, although, amazingly, there isn't even a need for windshield wiper controls. Sensors in the windshield that measure the size and intensity of raindrops can control the wipers.

Take a close look. This may offer a portrait of things to come.

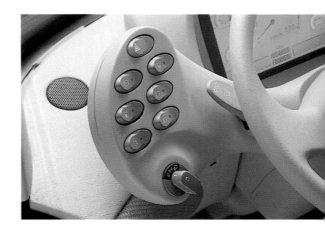

ABOVE Fingertip controls are within easy reach on instrument pods.

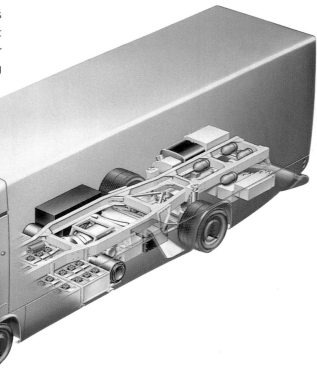

BELOW Powered electrically in the city, the ECT can switch to ethanol or other alternative fuels when traveling longer distances.

ERF: EUROPE'S BIGGEST GAS TRUCK
NATURAL GAS OUT OF AN URBAN SETTING

Natural gas is beginning to break barriers for a Belgian utility company. British truck maker ERF unveiled its alternative fuel solution in 1996 with a six-wheel double drive chassis and a drawbar trailer rig capable of a gross combination weight of 44 tons

for Electrabel—a privatized utility company that supplies Belgium with gas and electricity. Under the hood of the ERF EC12.34 DB3(G) is a 12.2-liter Perkins Eagle engine that delivers 340 bhp at 1,900 rpm. Building on the design of Eagle Tx diesel power, the 340 TxSi offers air-to-air charge cooling, a wastegate turbocharger, and two-way oxidation catalyst. And a drive-by-wire system electronically controls the ignition, air, and gas management systems. The result: lower NOx emissions and less particulate matter in a design that can already meet the Euro 3 Enhanced Environmentally Friendly Vehicle legislation for alternatively fueled vehicles expected in 2000/2001.

A ZF eight-speed synchromesh gearbox drives a Rockwell double drive rear bogie riding on ERF 2 spring suspensions. And in place of an engine brake, the truck is fitted with a Telma electronic retarder.

On the road, the truck incorporates hook-system demountable bodies and a 20-ton crane on a 26-ton gross chassis that carries cable drums or maintenance supplies. The trailer incorporates an 18-ton emergency generator. With its own cleaner power source, it helps move power where it's needed. "We have now passed through the phase where only urban delivery vehicles were considered to be candidates for gas power," said John Bryant, managing director at ERF.

ABOVE ERF has addressed many of the traditional shortcomings of natural gas, such as limited fuel capacities and short range.

FREIGHTLINER: THE PENTHOUSE
THE FUTURE OF LUXURY TRUCKING?

How comfortable can a sleeper be? That may be apparent in a concept sleeper unveiled by Freightliner at the Mid-America Trucking Show in 1997, which includes a 50-inch-wide upper bunk, or loft, that can be raised to the ceiling or lowered to its standard sleeping position at the flick of a switch.

Designed for Freightliner Century Class trucks with 70-inch raised-roof SleeperCabs, its luxury features include a flat panel display that can be used as a monitor for a built-in computer or a television screen and an integrated computer and entertainment package. A modem links the computer to the Internet, while mounting options allow the screen to be seen from either the bunk or the seating area.

A kitchenette located on the driver's side of the sleeper has a sink, refrigerator, microwave oven, coffee maker, and countertop and fluorescent lighting. Meanwhile, its water system is equipped with a fresh water reservoir, water heater, and a "gray water" tank. A pantry is also available to store food. Behind the passenger seat is a cabinet with a fold-down table, while the seat itself swivels 180 degrees to face it. A third seat, positioned on the passenger side of the sleeper, swivels and has a powered leg lift for added relaxation. Home-style 120-volt AC outlets allow standard appliances to be used instead of the dearer 12-volt DC items, while the inverter draws power from four isolated gel cell deep-cycle batteries.

ABOVE The Penthouse would tie together its computer with an entertainment package that includes a stereo and television.

JOINT VENTURE
THE FASTEST TRUCK IN THE WORLD

If the modified 1997 Century Class owned by Longview Diesel and Interstate Wood Products ever took to the open road, it would be due for a ticket ... if the police could catch it. In a 1997 test run at the world-renowned Bonneville Salt Flats, the modified diesel truck posted a record speed of 224.163 miles per hour. "We stepped it up a little bit," Interstate Wood Products president Don Lemmons says with a smirk. It's a far cry from the trucks the Washington state carrier uses to haul wood chips along the West Coast of the United States.

The 1,472-cubic-inch 16V92 Detroit Diesel Engine features 16 cylinders, four turbochargers, and two blowers working to develop 4,000 hp and 3,500 rpm. All of this power is channeled through a nine-speed Eaton Ceemat transmission. The truck itself has a wheelbase of 268 inches. The tires at the rear are B.F. Goodrich H4DX14.5-19, while 34.5 x 9.75-18 tires are at the front.

The team, who began their work with a modified Freightliner FLD 120, have improved speeds from an initial limit of 197.388 miles per hour, posted in 1992.

ABOVE No Class 8 truck can rival the Joint Venture's amazing 224.163 miles per hour.

MAN: HYBRID TRUCK 2000
THE POWER OF TWO SOURCES

Perhaps it's appropriate that MAN powers its hybrid L2000 with electricity. In some ways, it's a return to the roots of many truck makers that incorporated designs powered by batteries at the turn of the twentieth century. This truck, however, is for a new century, building on the F2000 range.

An electric motor is linked to a traditional driveline with a propshaft that connects the motor to the PTO (power take-off) of the manual gearbox. When operating on electric power, the motor drives the rear axle with the PTO mounted on the engine end of the gearbox. The PTO clutch and the clutch of the electric motor are closed, the diesel engine's clutch is left open.

With a maximum power of 57 kW at 240 volts, the engine offers 220 Nm of torque up to a speed of 2,000 rpm—a maximum road speed of 40 miles per hour, a range of between $12^1/_2$ and $18^1/_2$ miles, and gradeability of more than 30 percent, allowing the vehicle to move when fully laden.

For longer distances, the truck reverts to a diesel engine. Its driver simply hits a dash-mounted switch to start the engine, the diesel engine clutch is closed, and the clutch for the electric motor is opened. The switch between the two modes can be made when the truck is moving at speeds of up to 31 miles per hour.

Still, there are weight disadvantages that don't make electrical power practical in every application. The electric driveline adds 2,645 pounds to the traditional truck, with another 330 pounds for the electric motor and inverter, 1,587 pounds for the NiCd batters and their container, and another 727 pounds in attachments. The truck is also restricted to a wheelbase no shorter than $155^1/_2$ inches, although it can be fitted with a liftgate and various bodies.

But while there is a reduced payload weight, the dual-powered truck can maintain its operating range and payload volume, with the bonus of environmentally friendly power that allows the truck to creep silently down any urban road.

ABOVE Electric motors may offer a future in pick-up-and-delivery applications, but are thought to have a limited use in long-haul applications.

THE SUPERTRUCK
THE TRUCK OF DEFENDING CHAMPIONS

Harri Luostarinen found himself behind the wheel of a new truck in 1998 as the defending European Supertruck Champion. But the Caterpillar European truck racing team still felt it had a winner. The truck, powered by a Caterpillar C-12 engine and capable of cranking out 1,200 hp, is run by London, England-based Chris Hodge Truck Racing Development Ltd. Its 12-liter engine design boasts six cylinders and a four-valve head with twin turbochargers and a fuel system incorporating Electronic Unit Injectors (EUI). And while the engine is specially prepared for racing, it retains many components found in standard production models.

The FIA European Truck Racing scene may include configurations that will never be seen on the road, with routes limited to the circuit of a track, but it's here that engineering muscle can be flexed. Still, there are limits. The FIA regulations dictate that the maximum speed must be limited to 100 miles per hour. But it doesn't take long to get there. The truck itself will accelerate from a standstill to its top speed in 10.2 seconds.

The transmission is a ZF five-speed automatic with manual sequential facility, while the chassis incorporates a multilink suspension with coil springs and gas shock absorbers. And under it all, the 11,000-pound weight is carried on Continental tires.

It meets the need for speed.

ABOVE Europe's Supertruck series is one of the world's few racing venues for heavy truck designs.

UNIVERSAL TRANSPORT OPERATIONS
KINDER, GENTLER ... WEIGHING IN AT 204 TONS

Australia is the ultimate proving ground for a truck's strength, with combinations that eclipse the lengths and weights found elsewhere in the world. But when Universal Transport Operations of South Brisbane, Australia, looked for a rig capable of handling gross vehicle weights exceeding 200 tons, it also looked for a design that would be gentle on the surface of the road at the same time. The operation heralds its resulting "3B" truck combinations as nothing less than "the new world benchmark in road transport efficiency."

With a 550-bhp 3406 E Caterpillar engine under the hood of a 4964 HD Western Star, each truck pulls three pairs of Darwin-built Ostermeyer side-tipper B-double trailers and dollies. And when loaded, the road train hauls 150 tons of zinc/lead concentrate over 74 ½ miles between the new McArthur River Mine and Big Bong on the Gulf of Carpentaria.

The 28-axle, 110-wheel configuration has a gross combination weight of about 204 tons cushioned by a Neway AD-246 air suspension on three drive axles. Tri-axle groupings on each trailer and dolly run under the 180-foot-long combination that is 5 feet longer than a typical triple road train. And the force of the power is channeled through an Eaton RTLO 18718B 18-speed transmission that turns the wheels at a maximum of 52.8 miles per hour.

But the configuration is also meant to be a model of efficiency in a project developed by Universal Transport, independent design consultants, officials from the Northern Territory Department of Transport and Works, equipment makers, and a Road User Research team. The tri-axle configurations are meant to be more road-friendly than traditional tandem pairs of axles—spreading out the weight—and the

ABOVE Universal Transport Operations regularly pulls 165 tons of zinc/lead concentrate in this monstrosity.

size of the trailers was closely matched to the capacity of a loader bucket operated at the mine. A semi-automatic hydraulic tarpaulin system was created to ensure that the loads were totally enclosed during every movement from the mine to the ship. And with the long configuration, seven-pin electrical connectors had to be designed to handle 70 amps per pin, to ensure power for brakes and lights as far back as the rear trailer.

When it's time to refuel, the fast-fueling capabilities normally limited to off-road mining equipment are brought to an on-road vehicle with a Wiggins system that offers a fuel flow rate of 66 gallons per minute, compared to the traditional 4 to 5 $\frac{1}{4}$ gallons. With that, the truck can be refueled in about 12 minutes. Then it's ready to continue a truly heavy-duty job.

ABOVE The warning placard for a road train seems almost redundant, but still offers a warning for traffic approaching from directly ahead.

WILD THINGS
PUSHING TRUCKS TO NEW LIMITS

There are some things that conventional heavy trucks aren't meant to do, so the "Wild Thing" series of trucks has been built to do them instead. These modified trucks, created in conjunction with Navistar International and the Cummins Engine Company have completed an annual race up Pikes Peak, Colorado—one of the steepest race courses in the world—competed as off-road racers, and will now face the demands of drag strips.

The first of the vehicles was Wild Thing I, which participated in the famous Baja 1000 off-road race in the fall of 1994. That International 9200, powered by a stock Cummins M11 diesel engine, was the first Class 8 truck ever to compete in the event.

For the Pikes Peak Auto Hill Climb, there were different requirements. Wild Thing II is a modified International 8200 tractor, while Wild Thing III is a modified International 9200 tractor, and both of them are powered by modified Cummins N14-525E Plus CELECT diesel engines. Typically, the engines are rated at 525 hp at 1,900 rpm with a peak torque of 1,850 lb-ft at 1,200 rpm. During a climb in the Pikes Peak event, the engines raced at more than 1,000 hp, developing peak torques of 2,700 lb-ft. The changes in power, however, were accomplished only by modifying fuel and air handling systems.

Both Wild Thing II and Wild Thing III have set Class 8 records in the International Pikes Peak "Race to the Clouds," with times of less than 16 minutes. And it's a course that tests their mettle, with a 12.42-mile dirt track marked by 156 hairpin turns over a vertical rise of almost 5,000 feet. The course doesn't end until the trucks pass the treeline at the 14,110-foot summit of one of the highest of the Rocky Mountains. Wild Thing III set the pace with radar-recorded cornering times of up to 62 miles per hour and straightaway speeds of 73 miles per hour.

But the program isn't finished yet. At the end of 1998, engineers were preparing to unveil Wild Thing IV, taking a massive International 9900 to new limits as a drag racer. Who says you can't do that with a truck?

ABOVE Wild Thing designs have tested the mettle of both Navistar and Cummins engineers.

THE TOP TEN
TRUCKS THAT MOVED THE WORLD

Today's trucks bear little resemblance to their ancestors. And for that every trucker should be thankful. Barring the occasional sentimental favorite, what driver would turn in the amenities and power of today's cabs for something long since relegated to the scrapheap? Some of yesterday's equipment couldn't even hope to handle the loads that have become commonplace in a modern world.

But some designs manage to make an indelible mark during their time on the highway. They stand apart from the thousands of other models that shared the same roads. Still, it's a daunting task to "rank" the most important trucks of all time when you consider the ever-changing designs. Is the world's first commercial truck line more important than a design that takes the industry's efficiency to a new level? Should industry acceptance shown by record sales carry more weight than a particular technological achievement?

Although this chapter is entitled "The Top Ten," the following profiles—listed in no particular order—are merely meant to offer glimpses at a few of the trucks that made their marks in history ... and on the future.

DAIMLER-MOTOR-LASTWAGEN
DAIMLER-MOTOREN-GESELLSCHAFT

The list of trucks that built an industry would indeed be incomplete without mentioning the world's first commercially built truck line. Gottlieb Daimler and Wilhelm Maybach had already found success by increasing power and shedding weight from engines. And after Daimler-Motoren-Gesellschaft models were powering everything from an automobile to a boat, the pair returned to the drawing-board in 1891 to design a truck. Five years later it came to life on the lines of their belt-driven private car.

The first models featured twin-cylinder in-line engines mounted at the rear of the vehicles, although later models featured the engines mounted under the seat so drivers could more easily access their loads. The belt drive's components, meanwhile, were protected under the loading space.

The final drive consisted of pinions that engaged internally toothed gear wheels that were attached to the two rear wheels. Designed to reach speeds of up to eight miles per hour, 4-, 6-, 8- and 10-hp models could carry loads of 3,300 pounds, 5,500 pounds, 8,250 pounds, and 11,000 pounds, respectively.

A prospectus for the first truck mentions a twin-cylinder, in-line engine known as the Phoenix or Model N, as well as a rotational cooling system. The latter system saw water fed into the interior of a revolving flywheel and, after the rotation cooled it, it was returned by centrifugal force to the engine's water jacket. The design even made it possible to offer a heating arrangement with circulating cooling water fed through tubes mounted on the driver's box.

The prices for the first trucks ranged from 4,650 through 7,730 Marks.

THE MODEL T
THE FORD MOTOR COMPANY

It may appear strange that the name of one of history's most famous automobiles would find its way onto a list of the most prominent trucks of all time. But modified "Tin Lizzies" quickly became the most popular trucks of their era thanks to an offshoot industry that provided conversion kits which enabled cars to be transformed into trucks.

The Model T Ford first appeared in October 1908 with a 2.9-liter, four-cylinder, L-head monoblock engine with a detachable head, and a foolproof two-speed-and-reverse planetary transmission that made it ideal for light delivery work. By 1911, a commercial roadster was available for U.S. $590 and a van for $700, although the official models only made up a fraction of those used for commercial work.

Within only a few years, dozens of manufacturers were adding new and heavier frame rails and extra crossmembers to the cars, for heavier duties. Conversion kits usually included a lengthened chassis and side chain drive, which made a cheap one-ton truck from the workings of what was meant to be a private vehicle.

Ford's first purpose-built one-tonner came in 1917 as the Model TT, over a million of which were delivered up until May 1927, when the last of about 15 million Model Ts was produced.

By 1926, Ford had 51 percent of the U.S. truck market, when Chevrolet's established one-tonner couldn't command even two percent of the business.

THE "DEUCE-AND-A-HALF"
GMC

One of the most popular American military truck designs during World War II was GMC's 2½-ton 6 x 6 model dubbed the "deuce-and-a-half" in reference to the weight. This was the truck that moved an army, and about 560,000 were built by the General Motors division that became America's largest producer of military vehicles. (In an ironic twist of fate, the nationalizing of General Motors' Opel Division in Germany created one of the largest truck builders for Axis powers.)

The GMC deuce-and-a-half boasted 104-hp engines that worked with five-speed main gearboxes and hydrovac brakes.

In 1940, 6 x 6 versions included the CCKW 352, CCKW 353, and AFKWX 353 with and without winches, the latter of which was also offered with a 15-foot body. The model was also used as a basis on which GMC built 20,000 DUKW "Duck" amphibious craft.

The 2½-tonner's development didn't end with the war, however. GMC had a new 6 x 6 with Hydramatic transmission in service by 1951, and the DUKW's successor that tested in 1956 as the Drake was unveiled as an 8½-tonner in an 8 x 8 configuration.

THE T600A
KENWORTH

Early detractors of Kenworth's T600A aerodynamic truck design referred to it as the "anteater," and undeniably, with its long, sculpted snout it looked like nothing else traveling North America's highways. Nor was it meant to.

With its aerodynamic stylings unveiled in 1985, the T600A reshaped the way many truck designers thought about aerodynamics, and later earned the U.S. Department of Transportation's National Award for the Advancement of Motor Vehicle Research and Development.

It was 22 percent more fuel-efficient than any other competitor, Kenworth claimed with the launch of the truck. And with a 65,000-pound gross combination weight, the manufacturer recorded an average fuel consumption of 10.8 miles per gallon over 2,346 miles. With a 46-inch setback axle, it promised even greater payloads without a deep fifth wheel setting that would have sacrificed ride quality.

In making the changes, Kenworth engineers focused on the front profile, which accounted for about 75 percent of any truck's aerodynamic drag. The hood was sloped, corners rounded, fenders swept back, and headlamps tucked under the contour of the hood and fender. The bumper, made of polyurethane, was further refined to reduce aerodynamic drag. And with the front profile sculpted, the addition of an integrated cab extender helped close the gap between the tractor and trailer—a traditional source of turbulence.

There were other advantages to the design, too. The sculpted hood offered an unprecedented view of the road when compared to other conventional designs, and the steering gear's positioning ahead of the setback axle offered a 40-degree wheel cut for a turning circle that bettered that of both conventional and COE designs. Kenworth had changed the shape of trucking.

THE AC "BULLDOG"
MACK TRUCKS

There is no other truck maker in the world whose name has meant so much to popular culture as U.S.-based Mack Trucks. Indeed "built like a Mack truck" is synonymous for all things tough, whether or not the speaker knows anything about the trucking industry.

The Allentown, Pennsylvania, truck builder made its mark in World War I as British engineers dubbed their Macks "bulldogs" because of their toughness. Said one report: "In appearance these Macks, with their pugnacious front and resolute lines, suggest the tenacious quality of the British bulldog. In fact, these trucks have been dubbed Bulldog Macks by the British engineers in charge."

Chief engineer Edward Hewitt is credited with creating Mack's AC model, which was offered in $3\frac{1}{2}$-, $5\frac{1}{2}$- and $7\frac{1}{2}$-ton sizes, with 18 patents covering its innovations. With the radiator placed behind the engine, the hood boasted a look unique in the trucking industry when it was first introduced in 1916. Air was drawn from under the hood, forced out through the radiator, and then sent through screening at the front of the cowl. The design was even seen as protection from radiator damage that could be caused by accidents or the "carelessness" of Teamsters (members of a U.S. union) who felt motorized trucks were the death knell for horsedrawn businesses. The AC further featured several automobile design standards, such as a steering wheel placed at a more comfortable 45-degree angle, rather than the 90-degree designs still common in its day.

The engine had a bore and stroke of 5 x 6 inches and was rated at 74 bhp, governed at 1,000 rpm with a piston displacement of 471 cubic inches. The gear ratio in first was 3.21:1.

Pressed chrome-nickel steel frame rails were heat-treated for durability, while aluminum was used for the radiator tank, transfer case, timing cover, and engine crankcase. The pair-cast cylinders were also heat-treated, and the compacting of the metal led to a longer engine life. Drop-forged alloy steel, meanwhile, was used to make the front axle robust in any terrain.

Hewitt was uncompromising in his belief that any deadweight that didn't improve the efficiency of components should be eliminated. And the weight was shed. For example, by casting oil piping as part of the upper and lower sections of the aluminum crankcase and the front cylinder block, he was also able to rid the engine of the external piping traditionally plagued by leaky connections.

The AC's simple three-speed selective transmission was coupled with a clutch brake, while the chain drive claimed superior pulling capabilities over final drive.

Just like its predecessor the AB, the AC had an all-steel cab with an optional metal roof, making Mack the first U.S. truck maker that was offering drivers more than an exposed wooden seat.

THE LIBERTY CLASS B
VARIOUS MANUFACTURERS

The Liberty Class B—also known as the "U.S.A." because of the lettering on its hood—was one of the first trucks in the world to incorporate standardized parts, for ever changing the lives of people working in vehicle maintenance shops.

Allied forces in Europe had found themselves hamstrung by maintenance and repair problems in World War I, the world's first mechanized war, primarily because each truck design needed its own array of proprietary parts. By July 1917, however, specifications were submitted for a 4 x 2 truck that was going to be used by various branches of the armed forces.

The Society of Automotive Engineers (S.A.E.) may have been more than a decade old, but this was its shining moment. By August, 50 S.A.E. engineers had formed eight working groups to design the necessary components for a cookie-cutter approach to truck making. Prototypes with 144-inch wheelbases were built in Lima, Ohio, and Rochester, New York. The engine was a 424-cubic-inch, four-cylinder model with a block manufactured by Continental. Cylinder heads were made by Waukesha and pistons by Hercules.

Both prototypes were delivered to the U.S. Secretary of War in October and, by January 1918, widespread production began with 15 different companies contracted to build up to 1,000 of the trucks every month. There were 9,364 Liberty Class Bs built by Armistice Day in November 1918. However, when the war ended, the order for 43,000 more was cancelled, and many of its builders were doomed. But the names of other manufacturers such as Bethlehem, Indiana, and Stirling lived on.

THE TILT-CAB COE
DIAMOND T

Diamond T made its reputation with aggressive-looking, long-nosed conventional trucks complete with their chrome hubcaps and variable-rate springs. But it was with the Tilt-cab COE that the U.S. manufacturer earned the 1953 National Design Award for an industrial product.

There was the dip in the bottom of the side-window ventilators that was copied by truck makers for years. And both Hendrickson and International used the cab. But the main attraction was the way the engine could be accessed for repairs—a counterbalance replaced the need for a power unit to tilt the 723C cab.

Between 3,000 and 5,000 923C cabs (a different model of the same truck) were built every year for a decade, with the cab centered over the front axle, sporting a curving, divided vertical windshield.

The company was eventually sold to White in 1958, and the last Diamond T rolled off the assembly line in 1966. In the 56 years before that, however, the nameplate was carried on 250,000 trucks. White merged Diamond T with Reo in May 1967 to form Diamond Reo.

THE MODEL 800
FREIGHTLINER CORPORATION

Leyland James began his trucking career at the age of 19, so he was no stranger to the business when he took the helm of Consolidated Freightways. But when James searched company after company in the 1930s, he couldn't find a lighter, durable truck capable of offering a more comfortable ride to fit the needs of his fleet. It was a tall order, but he wanted a lightweight truck for heavy linehaul work that offered the maximum legal payload. For this reason his maintenance shops started building their own trucks.

In 1936, shops at James' Salt Lake City, Utah, facility were building aluminum trucks and trailer bodies, adding the first of the cabs to a Fageol chassis and a six-cylinder Cummins diesel engine in 1937. The idea was working. Under the name Freightways Manufacturing, the CF100 COE was released in 1940, and Consolidated Freightways took them all. The plant shut down in 1942 because of a wartime priority for metals, but production resumed in 1947 under a new subsidiary known as Freightliner Corporation.

The timing was a big help. Advances made in the production of aluminum and magnesium during the war were applied to the truck, making new Freightliners a full ton lighter than other comparable units on the road.

The Model 800, which was known as the "bubble nose," was the first in a series of custom vehicles made by the company. And in 1950, the first was sold to an outside customer. In 1951, White Motor Company became Freightliner's sales and service outlet.

The basic square cabs were nicknamed "Monkey Ward" Freightliners, suggesting that they could have been built with mail-order parts. But that first truck was the beginning of a truck-making dynasty. As a division of Daimler-Benz, today's Freightliner Corporation dominates truck building in North America, and has expanded its influence into other countries from Australia to China.

THE SPEED WAGON
REO

When Ransom Eli left Olds "for certain reasons" in 1904, there were hard feelings with the company he had established. But he had a different business philosophy than his business partners and the bank. It was time for him to launch a new brand.

After several successful launches, Reo advertised a ³/₄-tonner with the names "Speed Wagon" or "Hurry Up Wagon." But it was the "Speed Wagon" name that became its well-known moniker.

Even though specifications listed a top speed of 22 miles per hour—still quick for the day—those who used it claimed they could reach 40 miles per hour when the truck was fully loaded. The truck came with an electric starter and a 45-hp, four-cylinder engine with a 13-plate clutch and three-speed selective sliding gear transmission and bevel drive.

A two-ton Model J was sold for $1,650 without a body, but the engine was uprated to offer a model with a top speed of 27.23 miles per hour. About 19,900 Speed Wagons were sold by 1919, with body designs ranging from hearses to ambulances. And the name was attached to various Reo designs as late as 1939.

THE TRANSCONTINENTAL TRUCK
SAURER

Saurer brought Swiss truck designs to the world after designing its first truck in 1903, much to the credit of a wide-reaching business approach. At one time it boasted branch factories in France and Germany, not to mention the licensed plants in Vienna, Austria, and New Jersey, United States. And at the height of its success, the Swiss nameplate could be found from Russia to the far-reaching colonies of the British Empire. (Saurer is even credited with advancing diesel engine designs in 1908, under the watchful eye of none other than Rudolf Diesel.)

Four chassis of the initial truck line were built for payloads of 1¹/₂, 2, 3 and 3¹/₂ tons. The smaller two had 16-hp, four-cylinder engines offering speeds of about 15 miles per hour through a shaft drive, while heavier models were powered with a 30-hp engine and retained chain drive. Each design also had a four-speed gearbox.

One of Saurer's crowning achievements though, was using one of its trucks to make a transcontinental truck run in North America, traveling from Los Angeles, California, to New York, New York, in 1911. Many other makers followed, but it was the first.

THE TRUCK OF THE FUTURE

Volvo Trucks North America

ABOVE The World Wide Web is emerging as a virtual dealership, offering buyers the opportunity to gather information on a particular design or even spec' it.

WHERE DOES THE TRUCK GO FROM HERE?

No matter how far they travel or how powerful they become, there's something that the modern truck can't outrun: the information age. Engines controlled by computer chips, trucks tracked by satellites, and radar systems to warn drivers about the traffic around them were unimaginable a few decades ago. Today they're a reality.

Granted, these systems can't be found on every truck, even in regions where their use has been embraced. Electronic engine designs common in North America have yet to be accepted in Europe—and certainly not by emerging markets such as China, India, and Russia. Even when satellites are used to track runs from Europe to Russia, or throughout North America, their promise as tools for more than locating a load is only now being realized. But engine makers are finding ways to link their equipment to satellites and digital phone networks, making it possible to diagnose maintenance problems while a truck is still on the road. For that matter, problems that can be solved by re-programing an engine computer can be done without bringing a truck into a shop. The possibilities such technology holds are endless.

When looking at trucks that travel today's roads, there's also the obvious question of which shape will dominate the highways of the future. That's as much a function of politics as the realities offered through the designs. COEs are still preferred in regions with strict overall length laws and requirements for better maneuverability. Conventional designs are sought in areas where there's a call for ever-bigger engines, or when driver comfort is more of an issue because of a shortage of bodies to put behind the wheel.

But don't expect bullet-shaped trucks anytime soon, even if the idea seems futuristic. Whichever style wins out (it's doubtful that one will be accepted by every region of the world) there are practical limits to what bold changes to shapes can accomplish in terms of fuel economy. Indeed, today's designs are rounder and sleeker than anything that's ever traveled the road, and that means fuel savings for operators. A one percent increase in aerodynamic efficiency can return a half percent improvement in fuel economy when a truck cruises at highway speeds. But trucks will never be allowed to travel at the supersonic speeds of the Concorde, or even at the speeds of bullet passenger trains that make certain aerodynamic changes practical.

It's the traditional trailer shape that is a relatively untouched frontier in terms of airflow. There's some thought that a rig's aerodynamics could be improved by 40 percent simply by tackling these boxes on wheels. Perhaps we'll see a membrane that closes the gap between tractors and their trailers. Sculpting the rear of a trailer would deal with turbulence, but a tapered rear end would also require governments to allow a greater overall trailer length to offer room for the improvement.

As for the fuel that will run the trucks of the future, an array of power sources are being considered, from fuel cells to alternative fuel sources such as natural gas. But don't sound the death knell for diesel just yet. The most advanced designs available are still only 42 percent efficient. There's room for improvement.

Sometimes, however, the call for more power is louder than that for fuel efficiency—particularly in Australia. (Several engineers have told me that if they can build it, the Australians will buy it.) But current engine limits of 2,050 lb-ft of torque are held fast by transmission designs. This is the next barrier to be overcome if engines are to grow, perhaps requiring input shafts with larger diameters, and clutch and pressure plates growing in radical redesigns to handle the power.

In the final analysis, the most important questions concerning advancements in trucking are linked to the driver. What of him? Could he be replaced? It's unlikely that truckers will disappear, but their jobs are changing. The driver of the future will in all likelihood take on an increasing role as someone to monitor the truck's action and continue to offer a human face to deal with customers. Just think of the level of automation that's already come to such components as transmissions. An inexperienced driver can wreak havoc on a manual design. Even expert float shifters who work without a clutch can occasionally misuse the gears. Synchronized varieties popular in Europe may be closer to those of cars, eliminating the need for double clutching, but synchronizers can be ripped apart when they're misused. But now there are several "automated" mechanical transmission designs on the market, using electronics to measure road speed and decide when it's appropriate to make a shift, and leaving the clutch only for starting and stopping. Scania's EuroTronic, Meritor's Engine Synchro Shift and SureShift, and Eaton's AutoShift partially automated transmissions are just now proving their worth.

Meanwhile, cruise control was a godsend for drivers on U.S. Interstates, giving them the ability to take their foot off the throttle for long hauls at constant speeds. Adaptive cruise controls are the next logical step. In 1998, Eaton unveiled the first such design with the EVT 300 collision warning system linked to a Smart Shift option. The final result was a cruise control that also controls the throttle, engine brake and transmissions, keeping a safe space cushion between an Eaton-equipped truck and the vehicles in front of it, without the driver having to do anything but steer.

In 1997, the U.S. National Automated Highway System Consortium demonstrated future equipment that could make some jobs of drivers obsolete. With the right magnets and sensors in a road, trucks could control themselves, in conjunction with special equipment that registers the distance to the vehicles in front of them. Similarly have there been experiments through the European Road Transportation Telematics Implementation Co-ordination Organization (ERTICO), and in Japan. Future trucks could be automated to travel close to each other in high-speed convoys.

Such systems, however, are pipe dreams for the distant future. The cost of building such an infrastructure would be tremendous. Systems based within individual trucks are more likely.

Even when a driver needs to control a truck, sensors can help guide him in new ways. Freightliner has unveiled an experimental lane departure system that will offer a rumbling warning to the driver. Roll stability sensors could help tell drivers if they're taking ramps too quickly. Such warnings may appear second nature to experienced drivers, but dwindling pools of employees are making it necessary to consider which systems might make it easier to ease new bodies into the cab. It comes down to both the cost and the benefits.

What is certain is that the truck of tomorrow will have as much in common with today's trucks as a modern rig has with the first one tonners.

ABOVE Computer chips are emerging in the most unlikely places. Tire manufacturers are designing technology that will allow truck owners to track tire pressure and temperature, as well as track a tire through its entire life—such as monitoring the number of times it has been re-treaded, for example.

BELOW By incorporating engine brakes further into engines, such as this Jacobs Vehicle Systems design, there's the possibility of hydraulically opening valves even when a traditional camshaft won't. Such full control could lead to better fuel economy and cleaner emissions.

GLOSSARY

Every industry is bound to develop its own lexicon. Trucking is no different. But what exactly is a 6 x 4 tractor or a B-train? And in the more colorful vernacular of the CB, what does it mean if a cog-grinder spots a coop while deadheading to a beanery? The following are a few definitions to help you understand the meaning of truck-related terms found in different areas of the world.

10-4 A phrase used on a Citizens' Band radio to indicate that a message has been received.

6 x 4 The numeric description of a specific tractor configuration. The first number counts the total number of wheels and the second number counts the number of drive wheels. A pair of dual wheels is only given the value of one.

A

ABS An Anti-lock Braking System that uses computers, sensors, and valves to modulate the application of brakes if a wheel locks up.

AFV An Alternative-Fueled Vehicle, which includes any engine design powered by something other than gasoline or diesel fuel. Examples include CNG (Compressed Natural Gas), LNG (Liquified Natural Gas), electrical power, or propane. In most cases they're considered more environmentally friendly than traditional engines.

Aftercooler A device that cools a turbocharger's pressurized air before it reaches an engine's cylinders. Usually it incorporates an air-to-air heat exchanger mounted in front of or next to the traditional radiator.

Air brakes Heavy trucks typically use air-powered brakes because the systems can work at low pressures such as 100 psi. The compressor is able to compensate for small leaks, the system is flexible to install, and the brake systems on tractors can easily be hooked up to trailers (see Gladhands).

Air-ride A suspension system that incorporates air-filled rubber bags instead of steel springs. The compressor and air reservoir are common to the ones used to power air brakes.

Alligator (slang) The casing of a blown-out tire seen lying on the road.

ATC (or ASR) The Automatic Traction Control or Anti-Spin Regulation that automatically applies brakes or reduces the throttle to stop the spinning of wheels.

Automated transmission Unlike a fully automatic transmission, these transmissions are only partially automated, still requiring a clutch for starting and stopping.

AVI Automatic Vehicle Identification systems can use tags and electronic readers to identify trucks. They're used for such programs as electronic toll collections.

B

Bar A protective barrier mounted at the front of a truck to minimize damage caused by hitting wildlife.

Bark The loud sound made with the activation of an engine brake.

BBC A common expression of a truck's size, measuring it from the Bumper to the Back of the Cab.

Beanery (Slang) A restaurant.

Bill of lading The document that details the goods found in a particular shipment.

Bobtail A tractor traveling without its trailer.

Bogie (or Bogey) Two or more axles linked together, usually as a pair in tandem.

Bore The diameter of a cylinder.

BHP The Brake Horsepower determined through testing with a brake dynomometer.

Brake fade Lost brake power caused when brake components are overheated. More typical to drum-style brakes, it can be linked to hot linings and expanding drums. Typically, it happens when brakes are overused while traveling down a hill.

Bridge formula An engineering formula used to determine allowable weights and axle spacings.

B-train A rig incorporating two semi-trailers and a tractor, popularized in Canada and Australia. The first trailer incorporates two or three axles on the rear of a trailer body. The second or third axle extends from the rear of the first trailer and supports the nose of the second, without the need for a converter dolly (see Dolly).

Bud wheel A type of disc wheel with 10 bolt holes and a stud-piloted design popularized by the Budd Corporation. Disc wheels incorporate single-piece rim and wheel designs made of stamped and welded steel or forged aluminum, anchored by eight or 10 fasteners.

Bull hauler (slang) A truck loaded with cattle.

Bull-nose A trailer that's usually extended 12 inches to the front, with 45-degree cuts at the corners to allow the turning of the tractor. These are typically used with loads that "cube out" before they "gross out." In short, they run out of space before they run out of allowable weight.

Button her up (slang) Secure a truck's tarp.

Buttonhook A style of wide turn that allows for the tracking of the rear of a trailer.

C

Cabover A truck design most common in jurisdictions where overall length or tight turning radii are an issue. The cab of the truck is mounted over the engine in what is referred to as a Cab-Over-Engine (COE) design.

Cackle crate (slang) A load of chickens.

Cast spoke wheel A wheel with five or six spokes radiating from a hub. The spoke, usually made of cast steel, is bolted to a multiple-piece steel rim.

CB A two-way Citizen's Band radio popular among truckers for communicating from one truck to another.

CDL Commercial Driver's Licence.

COFC A Container on Flat Car refers to a highway trailer moved on a railway flatbed (see Intermodal).

Cog grinder (slang) A truck driver, or truckie.

Conventional A truck design with the engine placed under the "hood" in front of the driver.

Coop (slang) An inspection station, typically run by a regional department of transportation.

D

Dead-heading Moving a truck without any cargo. On the CB, it's also been called "hauling post holes."

Diesel engine An engine design that ignites fuel by injecting it into a cylinder with compressed and hot intake air, rather than the spark ignition typical to gasoline engines.

Displacement The volume of space swept by an engine's pistons as they move up and down their respective cylinders. It's expressed in liters or cubic inches.

Dog (slang) A slow-moving truck.

Doghouse The hump in the middle of a COE truck cab that offers room for the engine tunnel underneath.

Dolly The combination of an axle, drawbar, and fifth wheel that can link with the kingpin of a trailer, allowing several semi-trailers to be linked together.

DOT The Department of Transportation— a government body that regulates the use of trucks and other vehicles. The phrase usually refers specifically to the inspectors under its control.

Doubles A tractor and two semi-trailers, with the trailers linked by a converter dolly.

Drive axle A powered axle on a truck.

Driveline Components that transmit power from the transmission to the drive axle, including at least one driveshaft with a universal joint positioned at each end.

Drivetrain All components but the engine that transmit power to the rear wheels, such as the clutch, transmission, driveline, and drive axle.

DRL Daytime Running Lights are low-beam headlamps automatically turned on when the parking brake is disengaged and the ignition is turned on. Widely seen as a safety feature to maximize visibility.

Dynamiting brakes (slang) A full and sudden application of the brakes, usually caused when spring brakes apply because of lost air pressure.

E

ECM The Electronic Control Module, which acts as the "brains" of an electronic engine or any other electronically controlled device.

EDI Electronic Data Interchange, which allows information about a load to be sent from one computer to another.

F

Fifth wheel The plate attached to a tractor or a dolly, with jaws designed to lock around the kingpin that hangs underneath a trailer. Combined, they offer a point around which a combination can pivot.

Float shifting The art of shifting without a clutch. It's usually only mastered by experienced drivers.

G

GAWR The Gross Axle Weight Rating is the rated capacity for a suspension system. That includes the axle, the springs, the tires, and the wheels. The least-rated component will determine the GAWR.

GCWR The Gross Combination Weight Rating is the allowable weight rating for a truck, its trailers, and the cargo. Because a truck can pull more than it can carry, the GCW (actual weight) can even triple the GVWR (see later).

Gear ratio This represents how many turns an input shaft needs to make for every single turn of an output shaft.

Geared speed A vehicle's speed at a governed revolution in the top gear.

Gladhands The quick connectors used to link trailers to a tractor's air supply.

Goose it (slang) Step heavily down on the throttle.

Grinding a pound (slang) Missing or grinding gears.

Gross power The power determined in a controlled laboratory test with no accessories. An engine's net power refers to the actual power at the flywheel, with working attachments such as the fan, water pump, air compressor, generator, intake, and exhaust systems.

Gumbo (slang) Thick mud.

GVW The Gross Vehicle Weight is the actual weight of the truck in terms of equipment, occupants and cargo.

GVWR The Gross Vehicle Weight Rating is the allowable weight for the truck, including the truck's tare weight, occupants, and cargo.

Gypsy (slang) A trucker who will haul a load to any destination, and tends to work for an array of carriers.

H

Hazmat A load of hazardous materials.

Headache rack (slang) A heavy barrier behind a cab that prevents loads from shifting from the trailer and crushing the cab.

Horsepower (hp) A measurement used to determine an engine's power. A single horsepower produces 33,000 lb-ft of work in a minute.

Hours of service The number an hours a trucker is allowed behind the wheel or in other work-related functions.

Hubodometer An odometer mounted on the hub of an axle, which is considered the most accurate way to determine the distance a tractor or trailer has traveled. It's calibrated to the size of a tire and records distances in both forward and reverse.

I

Intermodal A load that's moved by more than one form of transportation, such as by highway and railroad.

ISO container A container meeting the dimensional standards set by the International Standards Organization to fit on a ship, either 20 or 40 feet in length. They're moved over the highway on rigs coupled to a container chassis.

J

Jacknifing Placing a trailer at a very sharp angle to the tractor.

Jake (slang) A common reference to an engine retarder because of the dominance of designs created by the Jacobs Vehicle Equipment Company. Other retarders include hydraulic versions linked to transmissions, or electromagnetic designs meant to slow the revolutions of drivelines.

JIT Just-In-Time delivery schedule, which allows factories to run with less warehouse space and inventory. Parts or other supplies are simply scheduled to arrive as they're needed.

K

Kidney buster (slang) The ride offered by a rough road.

Kickdown (slang) A quick shift.

L

Landing gear The legs that support a semi-trailer without a truck.

Lift axle An non-powered axle on an air spring suspension system that will raise and lower, depending on the need to distribute weights.

LCV (or EEMV) A Long Combination Vehicle (or Energy Efficient Motor Vehicle) is a design longer than a standard double combination, such as twin 48-foot trailers or triple 23-foot trailers.

Logbook A paper document used to record hours of service.

Lorry (slang) A British word for a truck.

Lowboy A flatbed trailer design with a low ground clearance, typically used to move bulky or heavy loads such as heavy construction equipment.

LTL A Less-Than-Truckload load usually involves less than 10,000 pounds of freight. It's typically moved by a rig hauling loads for several different customers.

Lugging An engine producing too little power because a trucker has failed to downshift when the engine speed dropped below the normal operating range.

Lumper (slang) An individual hired to unload freight.

O

Overdrive The gearing in which the input shaft can turn the output shaft with less than one turn.

Owner-operator Someone who owns and drives his own truck, typically owning between one and four power units. Also known as an owner-driver.

P

P&D Pick-up and Delivery.

Peddle run A run using frequent delivery stops.

Pig tail The coiled cord that transmits power from a tractor to a trailer.

Progressive shifting A fuel-efficient way to shift a transmission that involves shifting before the engine reaches its maximum governed rpm (see later).

PTO A Power Take-Off that transmits engine power to auxiliary equipment.

Pusher axle A non-powered axle that sits in front of a drive wheel.

R

Reefer A refrigerated and insulated trailer used to haul temperature-sensitive loads such as perishable foods.

Rig The complete combination of a tractor and trailers or semi-trailers.

Road train A configuration that couples multiple trailers to a power unit.

Rocky mountain doubles A vehicle combination that has a lead trailer longer than the one that follows it. The overall length is smaller than that of a turnpike double (see later).

rpm The revolutions per minute of an engine.

Runaway ramp An area at the bottom of a steep grade, usually several hundred feet long and filled with soft gravel, which is used by trucks that have lost braking power. It's typically positioned on an upward slope.

S

Scrub Scuff-like wear on the side of a tire.

Semi-trailer A trailer that only has axles at its rear. The other end of the trailer is supported by the tractor's fifth wheel, a dolly, or the trailer's landing gear.

Shaking hands with the sticks (slang) Letting go of the steering wheel to operate an older two-stick transmissions.

Slider A tandem axle suspension that can move back and forth under the rear of a semi-trailer to redistribute weights or maneuver around tight corners.

Smokey (slang) A highway patrolman, usually identifiable with a Stetson-style hat also worn by Smokey the Bear—a cartoon character used to discourage practices that lead to forest fires. Also known as County Mounties when the police officers are linked to a specific U.S. county.

Spec'ing (slang) A phrase that refers to specifying a particular component or series of components in a truck's overall design.

Speedability The top speed of an engine determined by its power, the governed speed, gears, weight, driveline efficiency, air resistance, grade, and the load.

Steer axle The axle located at the front of a truck that's controlled by the steering wheel.

Stroke The distance traveled by an engine's piston.

Synchronized transmission A transmission design popularized by European manufacturers that equalizes the speed of gears without the need to double clutch.

T

Tachograph A device that incorporates a stylus to record the operation of a truck. Such a device records details on wax paper to track hours of service in Europe.

Tag axle A non-powered axle that sits at the rear of a tractor. Also called a trailing axle.

Torque Twisting force expressed in lb-ft or Newton-metres.

Trailer A load carrier that is supported by its own axles. A drawbar is connected to the pintle hook on the towing vehicle.

Tridems A group of three axles on a semi-trailer, in a configuration popular in Europe.

Trucker (or truckie) The driver of a truck.

Turbocharger A device that delivers pressurized outside air to the cylinders. The development helped diesel engines break the 250-hp barrier.

Turnpike double A vehicle combination common on turnpikes in the eastern United States, typically with nine axles and an overall length of more than 100 feet. Each trailer is 40 to 48 feet long.

Twin screw Two powered axles working in a tandem arrangement.

V

Van trailer A box-like trailer design.

W

Walking beam A suspension design with a beam placed on each side of the chassis, pivoting at the center, with the front connected to one axle and its rear connected to the other axle.

Wheelbase The distance measured from the center of one axle to the center of another.

Wiggle wagon (slang) A triple-trailer combination so-named because of the tracking tendencies of rear trailers.

WIM Weigh In Motion technology that allows a vehicle's weight to be determined without having to stop at a particular scale.

Y

Yard mule (slang) A tractor used to move trailers around a terminal's yard or warehouse.

BIBLIOGRAPHY

Brownell, Tom and Ertel, Patrick W., *International Truck Color History*, Krause Publications Inc., Osceola, Wisconsin, 1997

Craig, Andy, *Trucking: A History of Trucking in British Columbia Since 1900*, Hancock House Publishers Ltd, Saanichton, B.C., 1977

ERF (Holdings), *60 Years On: The Story of ERF, A British Commerical Vehicle Manufacturer*, ERF (Holdings) plc., Sandbach, England, 1993

Georgano, GN, *The Complete Encyclopedia of Commercial Vehicles*, Krause Publications, Inc., Osceola, Wisconsin, 1978

The Golden Years of Trucking: Commemorating 50 Years of Service by the Ontario Trucking Association, Ontario Trucking Association, Rexdale Ontario, 1977

Ingram, Arthur, *Trucks of the World Highways*, Blandford Press Ltd, Poole, England, 1979

Montville, John B., *Bulldog: The World's Most Famous Truck*, AZTEX Corporation, Tucson, Arizona, 1979

Mroz, Albert, *The Illustrated Encyclopedia of America Trucks and Commercial Vehicles*, Krause Publications, Iola, Wisconsin, 1996

Nicholson, Debi, *A History of the Future of Trucking*, Freightliner Corporation, Portland, Oregon, 1996

Olsson, Christer, *Volvo*, Norden Publishing, St Galeu, Switzerland, 1996

Schildberger, Dr.-Ing Friedrich, *History of Mercedes-Benz Motor Vehicles and Engines*, Daimler-Benz Aktiengesellschaft Stuttgart-Unterturkheim, Stuttgart-Bad Cannstatt, Germany, 19??

Siefkes, Doug, *Kenworth: The First 75 Years*, Documentary Book Publishers, Seattle, Washington, 1998

Thomas, Alan, *Leyland Heritage*, Temple Press, Feltham, England, 1984

Wagner, Rob L., *Kings of the Road, A Pictorial History of Trucks*, Friedman/Fairfax Publishers, New York, New York, 1997

INDEX